UP *from* ASHES

Rising from DEVASTATION to SUCCESS in Life and Business

By Jack Welch

With Susan T. Hessel *and* Gayda Hollnagel

xulon PRESS

Endorsement

It is a real pleasure to have the opportunity to write an endorsement for a book written by a man who has completely committed his life to Jesus Christ as he worked his way through a catastrophe planned by an arsonist to destroy him. Mr. Welch was one of the first pioneers to be able to design and mass produce homes on an assembly line type of production. At the time of the fire his business was capable of producing five homes a day. The author lost $19 million dollars that day.

The book begins with his life on a small apple orchard farm in a small town called La Crescent, Minnesota about 150 miles south of Minneapolis, MN on the Mississippi river. Here he recalls the hard work involved in maintaining a small farm and the struggles of the family as they work through rural life issues including their creative idea to build one of the first septic system and flush toilet in the area. The author is very honest and open about some of the humorous mistakes he and his father made including some the problems he had caused.

For readers who have questioned their faith–this is a very inspirational and encouraging book. He gives credit first to his Lord Jesus Christ, and then his supporting wife and friends for opening up the doors enabling him to **"Rise up From Ashes"** to his position in life today–very comfortable in retirement. One of the amazing things about the huge fire was the survival of his Bible–the only thing to survive the fire. His courage and ability to rebound and rebuild his life at the age of 52, is a very convincing and persuasive story. His banker and financial supporter said it best after agreeing to refinance the author who had lost all of his business and financial resources, "your integrity is your greatest asset". It was a good investment–repaid in three years and the beginning of Metrohome Corporation which had profits ten times greater than CBS homes.

Psychologist, author of the book **Psychoeducational Diagnosis of Exceptional Children,** professor at NIU–Northern Illinois University and an administrator of a research and demonstration center and professor at UI–Indiana University.
Dr. Milton Wisland

Dedication

For family, for faith, for friends, and for all those
who have ever sought more
meaning in their lives.

I challenge the reader: how would you
handle life's unique situations?

Contents

Introduction

S leep is all I could think about after working until almost midnight preparing for the next day's sales meeting. Between the two businesses—CBS Homes and Wright Homes—we had 120 people working for us in our three and a half acres of facilities under roof. We had become such a leader in component and pre-cut housing that we had just been interviewed for feature stories in two national trade journals.

Our future seemed so very bright when I went home and quickly fell into a deep sleep interrupted by a ringing telephone at 2:00 a.m. My wife Jann answered the phone. "Jack, there's a fire at CBS Homes," she said, handing me the phone.

I was so groggy, but I remember saying to Jann—maybe to convince myself, too—that it was probably just a paper fire, nothing significant. Dispatcher Katie Moore, who I knew, described a far different situation. "You better get down here, Jack. Your whole place is on fire."

In shock and with dread, I threw on clothes and ran outside that morning of January 17, 1980. Any hope of just a paper fire ended when I looked up at the brazen-red sky. At that moment, I knew CBS Homes had it.

As the *La Crosse Tribune* reported, the fire engulfed our office, component plant and roof-truss plant. The flames shot up hundreds of feet in the air and could be seen as far as La Crosse, Wisconsin, about three miles away on the other side of the Mississippi River. By the time I arrived at CBS Homes in La Crescent, Minnesota, it was clear that everything was bright except our future.

Family and friends surrounded me throughout the night as I literally watched my twenty-five years of work go up in smoke. When I first arrived, I asked firefighters to rescue as many records as they could, but none were recovered. I wanted so badly to get inside my office that it took several friends to hold me back. I knew that night that the biggest loss was not the building and equipment but all of our company records, including the 2,000 design plans that had been created over twenty-four years of business. All were in one room of the office building that I could not reach.

Sadly, we had talked just before the fire about making copies of those plans in case something bad happened, but we never did. We always put off making copies because we were so certain that it would never happen. Now we had nothing.

"We can always replace the building, but all of the years of plans are gone, gone up in smoke," the Tribune quoted me as saying that night. "What do we do now?"

This Fire Took Everything!

Water was everywhere from the two days that fire trucks poured water on this truly horrific fire. All we had left were three-plus acres of ashes from what had been La Crescent's biggest employer. Everything was reduced to six inches of ashes. There was eerie silence as Jann and I with another couple approached the barren sea of ashes. Each step of my boots stirred the ashes like puffs of moon dust.

My life in business flashed before me and an empty feeling followed. I felt worthless. I was shocked and overwhelmed. We continued walking through the ashes. Then my eyes noticed an eighteen-inch high and three-foot square area that was higher than the rest.

I bent down, reached under the raised area and pulled out a piece of ceiling insulation that had fallen onto what was left of my desk. Much to my amazement, the bottom of the third drawer contained my Holy Bible, and it was unscathed by fire.

The Bible looked new. It had no watermarks, smoke damage, or smell of fire. Around the perimeter of the

Bible was the charred remains of the bottom of that third drawer.

It Was a Miracle! God Had Protected His Word!

My office was twelve-feet by twenty-four feet with my desk and credenza at one end. The room also held our boardroom table. Thirty-five plaques and awards on one twenty-four-foot wall represented my years of serving on various committees and organizations and the honors that came with those positions. All those plaques were gone. The symbolism was clear. No matter what you do in life, it all melts to nothing except for the Bible, which is God's Holy Living Word. As difficult as the coming months and years were, that Bible convinced me that I would rise from the ashes. As you will read, I had success in life. But I do not write about it to brag or make myself appear important. I was an imperfect man—as I still am—but once I allowed the Lord to enter my life, and I became God's servant, everything changed.

This is the Bible that somehow survived the fire and inspired the changes in me.

Chapter 1

My Family History

L ike so many families, ours came to the United States in search of a better life. My great grandparents, Frederick and Mary Ann Welch, were teachers in Norwich, England—Frederick at a boys' academy and Mary Ann at a young ladies' seminary. Frederick was born in about 1821 in Lincolnshire, England, one of seven sons. Four emigrated from England: John went to Mobile, Alabama; Phillip went to Australia, and Thomas to New Zealand. William, Boucher, and Alfred stayed in England.

Mary Ann Wiley Welch was born on October 25, 1823, one of six children: William, Fredrick, Mary Ann, Alfred, Emily, and John.

The year of their arrival in Ohio differs in accounts— it was 1851,[1] 1852,[2] or 1853.[3] As one story went, after paying for a herd of sheep, Frederick went looking for farmland, leaving the sheep with someone he thought would look after them for him. When he returned, the caretaker and sheep had disappeared, along with his money. I can only imagine how disheartening that was. Frederick and Mary Ann felt their chances would be better out West—which by definition then included the Minnesota territory, just opening for settlement. They took their few belongings on a riverboat down the Ohio River and another up the Mississippi to Winona, Minnesota. From there, Fredrick rode his horse around the territory, looking for a place to buy.

He found it in 1858 in the area called Pine Creek outside of what later would be called La Crescent, Minnesota. As great Aunt Emily Welch told the story, the road to their land was so primitive that my great grandmother said; "She would never go over it again". Although the Pine Creek Road was an improvement over impassable mud or dirt roads, it was a corduroy road, which meant it was extremely rough. The road was composed of sand-covered logs placed beside each other perpendicular to the road's direction. Not only was it bumpy, horses could stumble if the logs rolled under the sand.

The Welch's arrived in the area that became La Crescent just seven years after the first settler, Peter Cameron, set up a trading post and a year after it was incorporated as a village called Cameron's. Peter Cameron was one of those early American characters about whom legends are created. Originally from New York, he first settled across the river in La Crosse,

Wisconsin, as a fur trader and frontier entrepreneur. He also built a saw mill and shingle factory. After moving to La Crescent, he wanted to make his new city the dominating community, not the one across river. So he worked to dig a canal that would divert the Mississippi River to what is La Crescent today to make it the main riverboat stop instead of La Crosse. Cameron died while building a saw mill in La Crosse in 1855, about ten weeks before the river bypass was to be finished. It never was, and La Crosse remained the larger of the two cities sitting across the river from each other.

One other note about Cameron was that he married a woman, Emma Eastman, who had a propensity to marry early and often. Cameron was her fourth husband by age twenty-two—her first was at age thirteen. She stayed with Peter until his death, but then went on to more marriages. As La Crosse Tribune reporter Geri Parlin wrote, "By the time she died, she was Emma (Eastman) (Kellogg) (Vin Sickle) (Cunningham) (Cameron) (Bowles) (Sharp) (Vin Sickle) (Spence) Wilson. And that's just the nine husbands for which records could be found."[4]

The *La Crosse Morning Chronicle* once described Emma as the most beautiful woman in La Crosse County. "The judgment of pioneers was that Emma was the handsomest woman that ever has been or ever will be seen in La Crosse, no matter how long it may endure or how great it grows."

John Welch's sawmill and water tower is in the back and E. B. Webster's House is on the corner. This photo, courtesy of La Crescent Historical Society, looks south to Walnut Street. Main Street goes to the right in front of the houses.

Cameron's was briefly called Manton by the developers, William and Harvey Gillett, and then was renamed La Crescent by the Kentucky Land Company. That name, which stuck, referred to the crescent shape of the Mississippi River around the town, which was incorporated in 1857. "The natural advantages of the location of this village are most admirable," according to a description in the *History of Houston County*, a book published in 1881 by the Minnesota History Company.

These nineteenth-century times were challenging for many reasons, including the risk of infectious diseases that we don't think about as much today. My great grandfather died in 1867, along with his oldest son, William, of typhoid fever. It was described as the "scourge" or plague of the nineteenth century. Alfred recovered from the disease, which is passed via contaminated food and water.

Great Aunt Emily's house in La Crescent. Emily lived on the second floor as she rented out the first floor for the income. She entered by the door on the right side of the porch, taking the steps up to her quarters. La Crescent Area Historical Society photo.

"Mary Ann was a widow with five children; the oldest was twelve, and they lived in an unsettled land where Indians came up the trail," wrote Great Aunt Emily. "One day an Indian woman came up the trail, toting a deer. An Indian man stopped at Great Grandma's as she had been baking bread, and he pointed at the fresh loaves and wanted some. She wrapped two loaves in a clean cloth and gave them to him just to have him leave. How did she ever take care of a family alone in those days?"

Early La Crescent Industry

The La Crescent area had some early industry, including the W. Smith Grubber Co., which produced stump pullers—or what were known as "grubbers." This important industry used pulleys and ropes pulled by a horse to clear stumps and land in a way that was much safer than dynamite and easier than digging.[5] The Company's stone buildings lie beneath Highway 16/61 where the stoplight is located, according to Donna Christoph Huegel, author of *Stealing the Mississippi River: Fascinating History of La Crescent*.

Huegel's book also mentioned the La Crescent Female Seminary, which served between twenty and thirty students, beginning in 1861. It was taught by Mrs. Rice, her son Edward, and a Mrs. Anderson. First names of women were not commonly used in those days.

Also in the twentieth century, the La Crescent Canning Company served the farming community, especially the fruit farms that were abundant in the area, about forty at its peak primarily with apple orchards. La Crescent was dubbed the Apple Capital of Minnesota, a title it still claims. Three of the sons of Fredrick and Mary Ann worked on fruit farms and orchards that became prevalent in their time.

The La Crescent Canning Company in 1912, where peas, beans, tomatoes and corn were canned. This property later was the location of CBS Homes. La Crescent Area Historical Society photo.

An early stump puller now owned by the La Crescent Area Historical Society. My grandfather invented this machine. La Crescent Area Historical Society photo.

A Different Way for My Grandfather

Grandpa's career took a different direction than his brothers. He farmed on a part of Houston County called Pine Creek, which included forty acres of apples on hills west of La Crescent. However, his income and reputation mostly came from drilling wells and building windmills all over Minnesota, Wisconsin, and Iowa. As his family had sadly discovered with the death of my great grandfather and great-great uncle, having a safe source for water was critical for survival.

Among the most creative well drillers was my grandfather, who designed and built six of his own well-drilling machines out of timbers. A steam engine drove the trip hammer steel cable with its drilling bit deeper and deeper into the ground, about 160 to 600 feet deep, depending on the terrain. The well drilled into the aquifer, the geologic formation capable of yielding sufficient water for a well. Our aquifer is said to bring pure water all the way from Canada, a line that many years later the La Crosse-based G. Heileman Brewing Company used for marketing its Old Style beer.

After reaching the aquifer, water was tested and a pump was installed. Grandpa always built the windmill that pumped the water. Today these private pumps operate on electricity or gas engines.

Uncle Raymond Welch is second from the left and Grandpa John Welch is third from the left in this photo that shows how large the trees were when they were removed. La Crescent Area Historical Society photo.

This steam engine empowered the well-drilling machine and pulled it to where it was needed. La Crescent Area Historical Society photo.

23

The steam engine that drove my grandfather's drilling machine burned wood to create the steam. Sometimes, when they ran out of wood, they burned fence posts on the farm. I'm not sure how happy the farmers were, but if they wanted a well, they had to agree. Grandpa's machine was so efficient and his business grew so large that he built six drilling machines, operated by teams of men he hired. He drilled all of the wells for the Milwaukee Railroad in this area and municipal wells all over the area including La Crosse and La Crescent.

Grandpa married Jennie Bartlett on June 20, 1900, but she died of diphtheria within two years of marriage. She left one son, Arthur, who was born June 23, 1901. He then married Anna Bowman, who came to work for Grandpa as a nanny and a housekeeper, beginning when she was a teenager. He was twenty-three years older than Anna, but they married in 1903 and had five sons: Ralph (my father), Lester, Clarence, Gerald, and Herbert.

Grandma was so distraught after Grandpa died in 1940 that she moved to Minneapolis, where she worked as a housekeeper and was an excellent seamstress in a group home for the elderly. She eventually moved back to La Crescent, where she took in sewing for others. She was very well liked, hardworking, and respected by everyone. She also had a love of plants and flowers, which she shared with all.

*The well-drilling machine that my grandfather invented. La
Crescent Area Historical Society photo.*

I have limited memories of Grandpa since I was just
twelve when he died on December 12, 1940. He was a
stern man with a big handlebar mustache who didn't
talk to us much. When he did, he scared us. His one soft

spot was for kittens, which were always on his lap when he sat down.

One other recollection I have of Grandpa was going with him to the acres of land where he grew hay to feed his farm animals. After Lock & Dam No. 8 was built on the Mississippi River in 1939 to improve navigation, water covered his land. That meant he had to find another place to grow hay.

My dad worked for his father in the well-drilling business for many years. Dad told me about the horrific conditions they found in some of the farm homes where they stayed for several days, especially if they had to drill deep ridge wells through rock. The farmhouses were sometimes frightfully unclean and unsanitary. He saw wives allowing their dogs to lick out of the frying pan and then cooked eggs in it without first washing it. Maybe they had so little water before the wells were dug that the wives thought this would be a way to clean the pans. My father said they had to eat those eggs because they were putting in long hours over several days, depending on how deep they had to go to reach the aquifer. They had no other source of food. Their choice was to eat it or starve.

Dad Meets Mom

Dad met my mom, Dorothy "Tess" Abbott Tessman, when she arrived on the train from Hastings, Minnesota, to teach at the La Crescent Grade School. My dad had the task of picking up the new teachers at the train station at First and Sycamore streets in La Crescent. They struck up a conversation and started going out together.

As a wedding gift in 1927, my grandfather gave my dad a new home. It was also a way of thanking him for working many years without being paid. That house was across the street from Grandpa's home.

River Junction in La Crescent, where my Dad went to pick up the new schoolteacher—who later became his wife and my mother. La Crescent Historical Society photo.

Photo taken by Tessie's Father (Julius) a professional photographer.

I was just a little guy—probably around 8—when a man knocked on our door and asked to speak to my dad. He told him that we could no longer live there, as the bank had called the note my grandfather took out on the house. Bank foreclosure, all too common in the Great Depression years, was devastating. Grandpa had some kind of loan against the house, which my father thought was given to him free and clear. What made this story particularly hurtful and puzzling was that my grandfather was then president of the La Crescent State Bank, a position he held from its founding in 1912 until his death in 1940. Even the bank president and his son were not exempt from foreclosure. My father was rightfully livid and never forgave that banker.

We apparently were allowed to live in that house long enough for Dad to build us a new house on his forty-acre fruit farm. Dad bought semi loads of used lumber, plumbing, and heating supplies for the house from Minneapolis. My father was a very proud man. As tough as things were in the depression, he would not accept government help. So determined was he to make it on his own that he worked two or three jobs. In winter, when there was less work on the farm, he brought logs into the saw mill to be made into oak railroad ties. He also worked as a substitute rural mail carrier for thirty-five years.

Resourcefulness Needed, But...

Dad was a very creative guy, far ahead of his time. In those years, particularly if you lived outside of a city, you used your own resources to solve problems. If you were mechanically inclined and willing to work hard and take a chance, you could make life much easier—or sometimes not so easy by your own creativity.

In an era when most homes outside the city did not have inside plumbing, my dad drilled a well and built a water reservoir six feet wide and ten feet deep. The water reservoir was built on a hill so the water flowed by gravity. Dad then dug a trench seven feet deep and 600 feet long to supply water to our house and three chicken coops. Every spring we went into the water tank to wash it down and purify it with Hilex bleach. This cleaning prevented mold and scum from developing.

When I was a teenager, I asked some of my friends to help me dig out part of the hill to reduce the incline when we walked up the hill to turn on the electric pump. It did help.

To modernize our home, Dad built the first septic tank in the area. The septic system was a wonder in itself, constructed into a cylinder shape from twelve fifty-gallon barrels. Each barrel was thirty inches in diameter and four feet high. The top and bottom of each barrel was removed and the sides of the barrel were split and spread. He made one large tank about six feet from our house by connecting three layers of four barrels each. The size of the finished septic tank, which he and I cemented, was six feet in diameter and twelve feet deep.

We punched holes on the sides of the barrels to allow sewage to seep out. It was huge, just unbelievably large and unusual at the time because all of the farmhouses and rural homes in those days had outhouses. We had the modern convenience of running water in both the kitchen and our bathroom and miracle of all miracles, a flushing toilet. We did not have to use the chamber pot at night or run outside to use the outhouse like my friends.

One Saturday, Dad looked down into a three-by-three-foot manhole in the middle of the six-foot diameter septic tank and realized it was filled and plugged. While the toilet and sinks still worked in the bathroom and kitchen, he told my mom that we had to stop using the toilet because the tank was full.

With our minister, his wife, and three children coming the next day for their weekly chicken dinner with us, Dad knew he had to take action. He told Mom not to worry because he figured dynamite would open the holes in the tank through concussion, allowing the sewage to seep back into the ground around it.

Dad went to downtown La Crescent to find his buddy, Joe Strupp, who was knowledgeable about dynamite. Joe took one look at our blocked septic tank and decided it would take three sticks of dynamite. It would be perfectly safe, he told Dad, because a long fuse would give them time to run once it was lit.

Mom took my sister Cynthia and I about 500 feet away to the hill above the chicken coop where we would be safe and still watch the action. Joe wrapped three sticks together, lit the fuse, dropped it into the manhole, and they started running.

The explosion terrified me because I thought he had blown us all up. What we saw remains forever in my mind: The dynamite blew off the top of the septic tank, twelve-inches thick by six foot in diameter. It rose

31

powerfully; oscillating in the air followed by a tornado of black goo that shot up fifty to sixty feet.

"Oh Joe," my dad said, "I think the lid is going to hit our house!"

The lid and goo went higher than our house and then miraculously narrowly missed it on the way down. It splattered the thick, black goo—sewage—all over the west side of our white house. We ran down to the house and peered into the hole and found nothing but a huge V-shaped crater. Nothing was left of the barrels.

It was an amazing sight to see, and my mother became so infuriated. I never saw her get that mad ever again.

Cynthia sits on the lawn of our childhood home that my dad built and suffered the consequence of the TNT explosion.

It only got worse. When we went inside the house, we discovered stalactites of that same black goo hanging from the ceiling of the bathroom and kitchen. The concussion of the dynamite caused tremendous backpressure inside the pipes that caused the toilets and sinks to back up. Cave-like formations hung from the ceilings of the house in which we lived. Mom went hysterical; she was just distraught. I can still see her shaking her finger at my dad and saying, "What have you done, Ralph? You've destroyed our house! You ruined everything. I can't imagine why you did such a thing!"

Seeing the enormity of our black stalactites and realizing the pastor and his family were coming for dinner the next day, Dad said, "Tess, I don't think we're going to make this thing work for tomorrow. I think you better call it off."

It was an understatement to say the least. Needless to say, we did not have that chicken dinner the next day or for the next three months. My dad had some guys come over to help clean and fumigate the house. They scraped and repainted the entire house inside and out. Dad power-sprayed the outside of the house with the apple sprayer we used on the fruit farm.

The problems were not just cosmetic. When sewage hangs from the ceiling in the form of stalactites, the odor is horrific beyond description. Add in summertime heat, and the stench just about wiped us out. Dad put lime on the sewage, trying to get rid of that smell, but it was still there.

All in all, it took about three months to return the house to normal, which also meant Dad had less time for the farm chores that provided our living. If ever there was a time that my parents might have divorced, it was that Saturday's misadventure. Our house became the talk of the town with many people coming by to see what had happened. People came in their Model A's, Model T's, and even on horses to gawk at our misfortune.

Dynamite Was Once a Tool of Choice

Dynamite is feared today, but in early times farmers used it often to uproot a tree or boulder. A tool of choice in those days, dynamite could be ordered from the Sears Roebuck catalog or purchased in a general store.[6] It was that accessible.

My dad told two other stories about dynamite that demonstrate how prevalent its use once was. The first occurred years before our incident when the road between La Crescent and Brownsville, Minnesota, was built. At that time there were no gas-engine vehicles or Caterpillar equipment to efficiently remove huge rocks.

One unlucky worker had the job of bringing in a horse-pulled wagon load of dynamite plus the separate blasting caps that would set off the charges needed to clear the road area. The driver, sitting on top of the caps on the wagon, never knew what hit him. The wagon struck a hole in the bumpy road, which set off the charges and dynamite. As the story went, not even a shoelace was left of that poor soul, the horses, or the wagon.

The final story involved a La Crescent man whose business was moving houses from one site to another. For one job in La Crosse, he was told to take special care to make sure a new porch arrived safely with the house at its new location.

In jacking up the house on steel beams, they discovered a woodchuck had taken up housekeeping under the porch. The decision was made to "fix" that woodchuck by taking it 150 to 250 feet away and strapping a stick of dynamite to its tail. When the fuse was lit that woodchuck ran for his home under the porch. Boom! It and the porch went up in kindling.

Notes

1 Neva Houston County History, 1919, Auenson, La Crescent: "A History of Its Frontiersman," a paper for a college course at Winona State University. Undated.

2 As told by Aunt Emily Welch.

3 Family story.

4 Geri Parlin, "The belle of La Crosse: Ageless beauty Emma Eastman had men under her spell," *La Crosse Tribune*, Feb. 13, 2006.

5 Donna Christophe Huegel, *Stealing the Mississippi River: Fascinating History of the La Crescent*, 2006.

6 Remy Jette, "Dealing with Dynamite," Massachusetts Academy of Math and Science, http://www.scientiareview.org/pdfs/16.pdf

Chapter 2

A Tinkering and Inventive Childhood

I was born on June 29, 1928, to Ralph Oliver and Dorothy Tessman (Tess) Welch in Grandview Hospital in La Crosse, Wisconsin. Life-threatening disasters occurred to me by the time I was two years old. My folks told me how I learned to walk and loved playing in my donut-shaped walker with rolling casters. When my walker got too close to the basement stairway, I tumbled head over heels with my walker, landing head first on the basement floor. Grandview Hospital doctors diagnosed a severe concussion, but I recovered completely.

The Lord Saved Me!

My second life-threatening situation happened while I was eating popcorn when I was two. A kernel became lodged in my windpipe. My dad took me by the ankles and shook me to dislodge the popcorn. Pneumonia developed with a life-threatening high fever treated in the hospital.

The Lord Saved Me Again!

By the time I was old enough to handle a hoe, I was put to work on our forty-acre fruit farm, which had five acres of raspberries, five acres of strawberries, grapes on a side hill, and the rest apple trees. Many mornings, Dad woke me to help him hoe or plant. It was all done by hand until we bought a garden tractor and eventually a John Deere for cultivation.

Once I was old enough to drive, my dad decided to build my sales skills by sending me out on the road with a truckload of apples, probably about 200 bushels. He told me not to come back until I sold them all, no matter how long it took or where I went. I headed west to Austin, Minnesota, stopping at stores to sell the bushels of Macintosh apples wholesale. I kept going west to towns on the way to Sioux Falls, South Dakota, where I sold my final bushels for about five or six dollars each. My dad, who left pricing to me, was pleased with the money I gave him on my return.

In the summer of 1943, I was fifteen years old when it was time to harvest berries. I drove our Model A Ford

Back in the day, La Crescent shipped a train carload of strawberries each day. La Crescent Area Historical Society photo.

into La Crosse to pick up berry pickers at the old La Crosse Tribune building at Fourth and Main. Mostly girls, they helped us pick the fruit for a nickel a box of strawberries or raspberries. That was good money then. I especially enjoyed and noticed the attractive girls working on the farm. I was the straw boss—in charge but still working beside them. I had to keep them moving in their respective rows instead of wandering all over to pick fruit here and there so they could talk with their friends. It was important to make sure we harvested all the fruit instead of leaving some spots on plants here and there. After I drove them back to La Crosse, I rode the tractor and cultivated between the rows of whatever fruit we were harvesting at the time. Loosening the ground between the rows allowed moisture to be absorbed, which made for better fruit that grew for longer periods of time. At the end of the season, we gave a picnic for our crew of workers, thanking them for their work.

I knew La Crosse well because I went to Longfellow Junior High School in ninth grade and then Central High School in La Crosse because La Crescent only had school through eighth grade. In good weather, I rode my bike twenty miles a day to attend school. I hitchhiked if our Model A was not available in the winter.

When I was in ninth grade at Longfellow, I began taking trumpet lessons. Listening to someone just learning an instrument can be painful, as it apparently was for my mother and others. One day Mom told me I had to get out of the house to practice, so I went to the henhouse, where I thought I would be more appreciated—until those 6,000 laying hens molted—lost their feathers and their ability to lay eggs for a time. Infuriated, Dad announced there would be no more horn playing. To make his point that my trumpet days were over, he turned my horn over his knee and bent it into a U-shape.

Not a Perfect Child

Rocks were my downfall on a couple of mischievous occasions. We used to throw rocks for fun, including one time when I smashed a neighbor's picture window. I sat in the corner until my dad came home and spanked me so hard that I wet my pants. He then insisted I go to the neighbor's house to apologize, wet pants and all.

Another time, it was one of those glorious Saturday nights when the parents were doing their weekly shopping and the kids had time to be together without worrying about chores or homework. Maybe we were awaiting the weekly movie that was shown outdoors in town on a big screen. Some friends and I sat behind the elementary school on a bank that overlooked the highway. Probably in about seventh grade or so, we showed off our car knowledge by shouting out different makes of vehicles that passed by below. I have no idea what possessed me, but I got up and threw a big rock that I was sure would sail over the kids. Instead, it went further, bounding down the bank and onto the highway and into an oncoming car. We saw the car bounce wildly into

The Cook & Harris store in the 1930s, the scene of my crime. La Crescent Area Historical Society photo.

the air with sparks flying. Dirt flew and oil spilled onto the blacktop. We all scattered. I ran to where my folks were at the Cook & Harris store in La Crescent, slowing down when I saw my dad sitting on the front concrete slab. I joined him casually, as if nothing were wrong.

All of a sudden the driver ran up and asked my father if he saw any kids hanging around. He told Dad that someone had thrown a rock that ruined his car. "If I find the kid that did this, I'll kill 'em," I heard the man tell my father. I was terrified; afraid someone would spill the beans. But Dad said he hadn't seen any kids around there. Eventually, I confessed to my dad—I was due for a spanking.

The Gittens Store was where we went to listen to the fight on a radio like the one below. The store had the only radio in town. La Crescent Area Historical Society photo.

In My Free Time

Yes, I had chores to do, but we also had a surprising amount of freedom—sometimes too much time and sometimes not enough. We had not-enough freedom when our mothers called us in for dinner when we had more playing to do.

Back then, we didn't even have a radio—none of us did. So on the night of the second Joe Louis fight against the German boxer, Max Schmeling, my dad and I went to the Gittens Store in La Crescent to listen on the only radio in town. It was a battery-operated Atwater Kent, the most popular radio in the United States. The company produced the radio, which it sent to cabinetmakers who installed them in wooden boxes.

"His radios were of very high quality and reliability with strong customer appeal to the middle class. Kent's customers often bought another Atwater Kent radio to replace an earlier one that lacked the newer features,"[7] wrote radio collector Ralph Williams. Williams noted Kent closed his factory in 1936 rather than cheapen his products during the Great Depression.

The two boxing matches became proxies for direct war between the United States and Nazi Germany. Louis, who was a hero to African Americans, lost the first fight on June 19, 1936, bringing great sorrow to the entire nation and claims of racial superiority from the Germans.

The rematch on June 22, 1938, in Yankee Stadium in New York City had a different outcome. We rejoiced that time because Louis—our guy—won. Incidentally, after World War II, the two men became friends, which continued until Louis's death in 1981.

Without video games, movies, television, or even radio except on rare occasions, we spent as much time outdoors as possible, making our own fun. Each summer the twenty-five kids or so in La Crescent held parades or put on circuses. The parade consisted of each child pulling a Red Flyer wagon with a wooden homemade cage housing their pet cat or dog, who was decorated with ribbons and bows to resemble what we thought was a circus parade. Some kids banged on tin cans to create a band. The parade stopped at a neighbor's garage, the site of our circus. We collected a penny from each of the twenty-five kids to start the show.

The circus even included a death-defying act performed by me. Bravely, I climbed to the top of a garage roof with only an umbrella that I thought would be like a parachute bringing me down safely when I jumped off the roof. The moment I started down, the umbrella went backwards and I dropped like a rock. Later in life I learned what it felt to really jump with a parachute, but that is getting ahead of the story. When I leaped from the garage roof, everyone screamed and hollered as I fell and then did what any kid does in that situation—scattered. It is a wonder that I didn't break any bones, let alone kill myself. Somehow, I managed to get up and merely limp away. My pride sustained more damage than my body.

This Atwater Kent radio was similar to the type our family had. Photo used with permission from www.atwaterkentradio.com.

After he won the second fight again Max Schmelin, Joe Louis later became a hero for all of us. He was a role model for the US Army during World War II on this recruiting poster. U.S. Archives photo

45

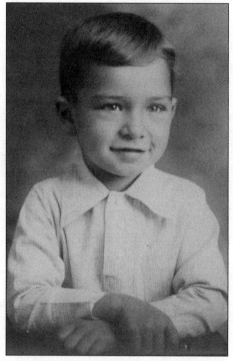

I was six or seven when this photo
was taken.

The Lord Saved Me Again!

It wasn't always easy to be a kid in the 1930s. When
I was about eight or nine, a kid a couple years older
than me terrorized me. One time, he threw my bike up
a tree, and I started crying, not knowing how I would
get it down. On another occasion, this kid ordered me
to take off my clothes and climb up on the beam of a
hay barn until he said I could come down. I didn't know
the word *bully* then, but that was precisely what he was.

Fixing Things

I always had an unstoppable belief in the ability to fix things even when very little. When I was about two and a half or three years old, I pointed to the half-moon one evening and said to my mom, "Mur, moon broken. Daddy, fick (fix) it."

When not being harassed by that bully or jumping from a roof, I liked to invent things, including a way to ride in my Red Flyer wagon without having someone pull it. I got into my wagon and pressed my feet to the back edge of the wagon and tied a rope to the rear wheel axel. I thought by pulling on the rope it would go forward. It didn't quite work out that way. What I was doing was an application of Newton's Third Law of Action. For every action like pulling on the rope in the wagon, there is an equal opposite reaction—in this case it is the wagon responding to my pull. I was always experimenting to learn why this happened or why something didn't happen or work.

My mom loved to tell a story from when I was in about fourth or fifth grade. I tied a long string from my mother's spinning wheel to all sorts of things around the house that I operated with pulleys. When I turned the spinning wheel, the string moved through the room turning things this way or that. My mother was not happy at the time with my inventions. "Jack, how can

I keep this house clean with all these wheels turning around the house?" she asked more than once.

Recognizing my mechanical ability, my dad gave me the greatest gift I ever received—an Erector Set. First invented in 1911 by A.C. Gilbert, it was manufactured by the A. C. Gilbert Company at the Erector Square factory in New Haven, Connecticut, from 1913 until the company's bankruptcy in 1967. Another company then took over the Erector name. The Erector Set was said to be the first toy in the country with a national marketing campaign.[8]

It was a thrill for me to build things with this kit because it taught me how things work. I built a huge crane without instructions; I figured it out myself. When I pushed a button, the three-foot-tall crane started up and could turn and pick up things like a book. With the Erector Set motor, I built cars, and I used the kit to build bridges and many other toys.

Freemasons

I remember as a boy my father sitting in front of our first radio—also an Atwater Kent—with the radio on high while he read the Bible, something he did every night. "Why do you have the radio on so loud when you're reading?" I asked him.

"I concentrate on reading, and I don't hear the radio," he answered.

My dad had a photographic memory. As the Grand Orator for the State of Minnesota Masonic Lodge, he memorized a complete Masonic book called *The Daggett*, which was printed in code on parchment paper. It was his responsibility to give lectures to new members coming into the Order.

Dad could talk for days just from memory, although sometimes he refreshed himself before he gave a particular lecture. I remember vividly when he was stuck on a word, he told me to look it up on a specific page, paragraph, and then something like the third or fourth word in. Once I told him the word, he went on again for hours.

The Freemasons, a fraternal organization for men, dates back to King Solomon, who was told by his father David to build a temple to God. References to the Temple were part of the Operative Freemasons—the Masons before their arrival in England.[9] In those early days, history in general was not well documented.

These traditions referring to Solomon's Temple continue to be part of the Operative Masons, who date back to at least the sixteenth century in England and possibly as early as the fourteenth. According to the Masonic Service Association of North America, the first four lodges in England in 1717 became the first Grand Lodge.

"Over the centuries, Freemasonry has developed into a worldwide fraternity emphasizing personal study, self-improvement, and social betterment via individual involvement and philanthropy. During the late 1700s it was one of the organizations most responsible for spreading the ideals of the Enlightenment: the dignity of man and the liberty of the individual, the right of all persons to worship as they choose, the formation of democratic governments, and the importance of public education. Masons supported the first public schools in both Europe and America."[10]

Presidents were Freemasons, including George Washington, James Monroe, Andrew Jackson, James Polk, James Buchanan, Andrew Johnson, James Garfield, William McKinley, Theodore Roosevelt, Howard Taft, Warren Harding, Franklin Roosevelt, Harry Truman and Gerald Ford.[11]

During my dad's time, the Masons provided a very important opportunity for men to socialize together. There is such camaraderie within the order that wherever a Mason is in the country, he knows he is always welcome in the local lodge or home of a Mason. The Masons are open to men of any faith, but some religions have their own fraternal organizations. The Catholic Knights, for example, limit its members to that faith.

Over time and through learning, a Mason moves up in the organization. Dad and I were Thirty-second Degree Masons, the highest degree you could obtain in the Masonic Order.

Freemasonry grew in the eighteenth and nineteenth centuries in the United States when there was very little, if any, government safety net. As a result, Masons built orphanages and homes for widows and the aged. Later, the Shriners, a wing of the Masons, operated children's hospitals, primarily for those with physical disabilities. Today, Shrine hospitals—including one in Minneapolis— serve such children's needs as burn treatment, orthopedic services, and more.

A Love of Flight

When I was about age sixteen, I began to design and build model free-flight airplanes. When many of my early airplanes crashed or went out of control, I figured there had to be a better way to build a plane. I took one of my homemade model planes to an event at the Winona State University football field. Up first, I asked another model plane builder to hold my model while I cranked the engine and turned the prop over a couple times. The plane rose straight up in the air and then dove toward the crowded grandstand, where people evaporated within seconds when they saw it coming right at them. The plane crashed, breaking into many pieces.

I had to find a better way to control the plane. After reading about the science of flight to figure out how to balance the aircraft in the center of the wings, I modified elevators, rudders, and wings. I attached a pendulum-stabilizing device that hung from the balsawood fuselage (the main body section). When the plane went into a dive after using up all the gasoline, the pendulum swung forward to operate control lines that brought down the craft to a safe landing.

Airfoil (the shape of the wing or blade) gave the plane lift and ailerons controlled the plane in a roll. The elevators ran the plane up and down off the tail, which gave direction through the rudder. My plane then climbed at a fifteen-degree angle without any change in course. I put a little curve in the rudder so it made huge circles and went higher rather than farther away.

On one flight, the wind current took over, sending my plane southwest over our farm to our neighbors. I saw this backwoods type sitting barefoot on his roof with his shotgun. He was shooting black birds away from his cornfield. When he saw my plane, he took aim, thinking it was a big bird. Luckily, I stopped him before he hit my plane.

When I was in high school, our family had a close encounter with another airplane. While eating dinner, we heard a rumbling in the sky above us. I ran outside and found a Navy Hellcat Fighter with a broken oil line circling to land in a cornfield on the adjacent farm. After he landed in the soft soil and just before hitting the fence, he applied the brakes and the tail went up and the propeller dug into the ground and came down to rest.

No one got out of the plane for what seemed like a very long time. Finally, he opened the cockpit. When we asked him if he was injured, he said he was just scared to death and needed time to calm down. When his engine quit, he knew he could not make it to the airport. He was fortunate that he had not landed on the nearby highway—as there were cars traveling on that road at the time.

One day a farm neighbor named Pete Krog asked me to mow his orchard, knowing our John Deere tractor had a side-sickle mower. When I finished mowing, he told me a story about himself that illustrated how creative farmers had to be in adapting to whatever problems arose. It also illustrates how mistakes could happen, as well as successes.

In this case, he had an apple sprayer pulled by a team of two horses. Pete had only one horse, so he borrowed another from a neighbor. Not realizing how unruly that second horse was, he hitched the two together and said "giddy up!" The horses did not move. "Pie Chiminey," this conservative German farmer said, "I'll fix 'em." He decided to provide some motivation to the horses to move by piling up brush under them and then lighting a fire. The horses moved forward a little and stopped. The fire did not—it burned up his sprayer. All that it left was its steel frame.

Growing up during the depression, I was always looking for ways to earn some money. So I took on delivery of the *Minneapolis Sunday Tribune*. I had to find my own customers, which I did, based on the rural mail route that my dad had. Very early each Sunday morning I delivered about thirty-five to forty papers, taking Dad's Model A on a journey of about twenty miles into the country.

In comparison with today, when subscribers pay by check or credit card, carriers in those days had to collect the money directly from their customers. They paid up, though. With so few forms of communication, they were happy to have the newspaper.

An apple sprayer minus the horses that once pulled it. La Crescent Area Historical Society photo.

Notes

7 Ralph Williams, "Atwater Kent: The Man and His Radios," http://www.atwaterkentradio.com/atwater.htm

8 http://www.erectorusa.com/

9 Bro. H.L. Hayward, Chapters of Masonic History, *The Builder Magazine*, 1924, http://www.freemasons-freemasonry. com/operative masons.html

10 The Masonic Society of North America, "History of Free Masonry," http://www.msana.com/historyfm.asp

11 http://www.mastermason.com/wilmettepark/pres.html

Chapter 3

Young Entrepreneur

With my interest in building things, I clearly was continuing a family tradition: the inventiveness of my grandfather and father. I had very large shoes to fill.

As a pre-teen, my friends and I built kid-sized houses out of used lumber left over from building our house. Some of these houses became fruit stands along the highway, but mostly we built them just for the fun of construction. We liked building so much that we tore a house we constructed down to rebuild it in a different way.

I was always the boss back then, giving my crew of friend's instructions for how to build these six-by-eight foot structures that were complete with doors and windows. I designed those houses to have proper fit for windows and doors, plus a roof and flooring.

We always put floors in the houses that were about two to three inches off the ground and were covered by two-by-fours and boards. We never considered what might slither under the floor.

I was especially proud one day when my parents and Cynthia joined me for dinner in one of these houses. We had a roaring fire in the stove inside the structure, where I cooked baked beans that I served on a little table. I was just thrilled that my folks would enter through that little door.

It all changed when we suddenly heard a frightening sound—like a crying baby—from below the floor. We ran outside to see what it was and discovered a bull snake with a wailing frog in his mouth that it was literally eating alive. That frog wailed in pain and fear. Snakes were all too common in those days and were always frightening. We ran away from my house.

Who knew then that the houses we constructed as kids were a forerunner to what would prove to be my career. I had what I call a gift—to build things and to lead others.

Jack in the Box

My creative dad, who always looked for additional ways to make a living, decided we should go into the crate-building business. Mom named it "Jack in the Box," a pun off my name and our product.

Businesses shipped big items in crates in the 1940s, not cardboard boxes. We had several large manufacturers at the time in La Crosse that needed crates built for their specifications—the Trane Company, which made air conditioning equipment; Allis Chalmers, which made agricultural implements; and Northern Engraving, which during World War II was honored for its defense work in producing 20mm cartridge cases and in recent years has made decorative aluminum and plastic nameplates, labels, panels, overlays, switch plates, sill plates, and trim for appliances and automobiles.

Dad traveled around the area forests and purchased standing poplar trees, which we cut ourselves. He put me in charge of estimating crate costs. I calculated each step—cutting the trees down and then into eight-foot logs, loading the truck, hauling the logs to our sawmill, sawing the logs into boards, removing waste, drying the wood in the dry kiln, sizing the boards with a gang saw, and actual construction.

Joe Shockley, a Jack in the Box employee, had the misfortune of breaking his arm at work. Joe came to my dad with his arm in a sling and begged him to keep him on the payroll. This was a time before worker's compensation or the Occupational Health and Safety Administration. If you were hurt on the job, you simply had to tough it out without pay if you could not work.

"OK, Joe. Jump in the truck. We're going to pick up some logs," Dad said.

When they arrived, Dad started the end loader and brought logs to the sixteen-foot-long truck box, while

Joe laid the first layer of logs. These logs were eight feet long, which is the width of the truck box. Each log was about eight to twelve inches in diameter.

When it was time for a second layer of logs, Dad and Joe placed two board planks over the top of the first layer of logs. These planks allowed the logs to roll easier for the tier. Joe did not realize the middle log was higher than the rest, which created an unexpected teeter-totter.

Meanwhile, Joe was standing on the downside of the plank near the truck cab. Dad dropped the next load of logs onto the high side of the plank. When the logs hit the plank, Joe catapulted 80 feet straight up in the air. His scream was heard throughout the area. Thankfully, Joe only broke his other arm, although with two broken arms, he was out of commission for quite a while.

While I was still a teenager, we manufactured chicken crates that were four feet long by two feet wide and eleven inches high. The top and bottom were wooden slats while the sides were composed of half-inch dowels. After studying the construction process, I developed and built a machine that sharpened both ends of the eleven-inch dowels. I then made a hydraulic press that assembled the dowels into the upper and lower frames. We built 1,200 crates per order, enough to fill a semitrailer.

In order to be more efficient, we also recognized we needed to improve our tools, including nailing and drilling machines and multiple-cut saws.

During the winter, when Dad sawed logs into boards at the saw mill, Neil Jore, another Jack in the Box employee, ran the gang ripsaw. Neil was guiding a board through the gang ripsaw when his mitten got caught in the feed roller. By the time he pulled his mitten away from the roller, the saw cut two inches into the mitten. Slowly, we pulled off his mitten hoping not to find a loose finger inside. Much to our relief and surprise, the saw cut between two fingers, leaving them without a scratch.

Thankfully, Dad was very creative in designing woodworking equipment. We built an automatic drill press that drilled holes on center all the way across a forty-eight by forty-eight-inch piece of plywood. Our press came down and drilled the entire sheet at once. That machine, which no one else had, meant we could build these crates more efficiently than other box makers.

La Crescent had many strawberry and raspberry farms, each about four to five acres in size. They produced fruit that was shipped all over the Upper Midwest. You can imagine all the fruit that was damaged by taking it down to the train station via wagon or light truck and then onto the train, where it shook all the way to Milwaukee or Minneapolis.

We started making crates for strawberries and raspberries that protected the fruit much better. To efficiently create these smaller boxes, I invented a stapling machine that ran off of a bicycle chain. It stapled the band over both ends at the same time, increasing our production 300 percent. We produced 1,000 boxes an hour, allowing us to sell crating through Minnesota, Wisconsin, and Iowa.

This business taught me a lot about being an entrepreneur while I was still in high school and college. You have to be willing to take big chances—including living without a paycheck as you start up a business. I believe there is something inside an entrepreneur that drives this success. Whatever it is inside us keeps us going, unable to give up. We keep working until we succeed.

When I was in high school in 1944, I was so tired of the long hours of hoeing in the fruit farm in the heat. I decided to build something to make the work much easier. I strapped a vacuum cleaner motor to a hoe handle. I then added what is called a worm gear and pinion to a 90-degree shaft with small rotating blades. A worm gear consists of a shaft that has a screw thread that meshes with a toothed wheel. That changes the direction of the axis of rotary motion and slows the speed of the gear while increasing the torque. With that, I could hoe my mother's garden in no time.

When my dad came home, I showed him what I had invented. He was so impressed that he took my invention and me to his engineering friend, who acted like he did not think much of the idea. A week later he and his family left town, and we learned he soon started the first tiller company in the country. Did he use my idea? I will never know.

Sometime later, Dad surprised me when he drove into our driveway on a self-propelled rake-hoe tractor that he invented. He took my idea and did it much better with this machine that he built over several months at Squeaky Hart's garage in downtown La Crescent. Squeaky was a small, thin man who was always creative in fixing things. He gained his nickname because in his line of work, he was always covered in grease. Thus, things squeaked by him.

Dad smiled from ear to ear when he showed me his invention, which operated by moving different levers and a motor that propelled the machine. Dad was clearly proud and excited.

"Jack, I think this will take us away from manual hoeing," he said.

I was the one who smiled the most. Hoeing was a boring chore in the hot sun that practically required us to work twenty-four hours a day. We used Dad's invention for about 90 percent of the hoeing. It moved well between rows of plants, saving a great deal of time.

We only hoed by hand when we worked right around the plants. I have no idea where that tractor went, but would love to have it today.

La Crescent Ski Tow

Around the time that we operated Jack in the Box, my friend, Dick "Ole" Olson, and I decided we needed a ski tow in La Crescent, which then had about 400 to 500 residents. We loved to ski and didn't want to drive all the way to La Crosse's Snow Bowl, which was south of the city where the current ski hill, Mount La Crosse, is off U.S. Highway 35.

We figured there were many people in La Crescent who didn't have the transportation to get to La Crosse but would love to ski if it were available closer to home. We decided we would build our own tow.

We first talked with the Snow Bowl operators, who told us that since they were going to buy a new towrope they would sell us their old towrope for ten cents on the dollar. It was still a very nice 1,900-foot rope. We then talked with a La Crescent farmer named Elmer Veglahn, whose property included a hill that would be just right for skiing. After we signed a release saying he would not be responsible for any injuries that occurred on the hill, he gave its use to us at no cost. That was good because we clearly had very little money. During the summer of 1945, we cleared the land of trees and brush with the help of a bunch of eager guys.

We then contacted a man named Melvin Hickenbothum, someone who made things happen in La Crescent. Melvin, who spoke like movie star Jimmy Stewart, said, "Oh, hell guys, this is nothing. We can do 'er."

About fifteen to twenty years older than us, Melvin suggested we get a Model A Ford motor from a junkyard in La Crosse owned by Max Bemel. Bemel had just what we needed in his yard and was willing to sell it for scrap prices. The car that once held it had been damaged in an accident, but its engine and transmission were still usable.

We loaded the engine and transmission and took it to La Crescent's last blacksmith—a man who still repaired farm equipment and shod horses. When we told him we didn't have a lot of money, he offered to create a frame and weld it together on a Saturday, which allowed him to just throw in his time. There was a hitch—we needed a second transmission, or it would run too fast. We picked one up at the same junkyard.

The blacksmith welded a frame to hold the engine and transmissions and installed a groove pulley through which the rope ran. We also built a V-shaped structure with old telephone poles at the top and a pulley system that controlled the 1,900-foot continuous rope as it moved. One skill I gained through this experience was splicing a rope, something that was critical to maintain a continuous towrope.

We were all excited to see this thing work. When we started the engine the first time, we were all smiles. We took it up to Mr. Veglahn's hill in the summer, staked it into the ground and started it going. When the snow came, we were ready for business.

Mel suggested a "Get Acquainted" Dance, to publicize the ski tow and raise money for the La Crescent Ski Club. More than 200 people came to that dance in the Commodore restaurant from all over the area. The two-dollar-per-person cost was comparable to about $19.30 in 2013 dollars, according to www.measuringworth.com. The money we raised that night paid for the engine, parts from the blacksmith, the rope, and other needs.

This was not a lift; it was a towrope. You held on to the rope in front and behind you as it pulled you up the hill. Your skis were on the ground the whole time.

We worried about whether anyone would come to the hill, but the first day was just unbelievable—people were so eager to ski that they waited in lines three blocks long. At fifty cents a day ($4.84 in 2013 dollars) per customer, we made between $300 and $400 dollars a day ($2,900 to $3,870 in 2013 dollars), which was a lot of money then. It all went into the club's bank account.

Ole and I had a great time. We managed the hill and responded if someone had trouble.

It all ended in 1950 after I was drafted into the Army. We had no one to run the ski tow so we donated it to the Boy Scouts, along with $6,000 that we had in the bank (about $58,000 in 2013 dollars).

Sadly, someone destroyed our equipment by using it for target practice. The Scouts also went through the money quickly. It was an important lesson for me that it is far better to earn what you get, rather than have it handed to you.

Incidentally, Melvin, along with Ralph Jones, was the founders of La Crescent's Apple Festival in 1949, which promoted the city and put La Crescent on the map. Clearly, he was a man who made things happen for us— and the community in general.

Coming of age at the time the United States was in World War II, I saw many young men around me leave high school to join the military. Due to graduate in 1946, I decided to finish high school and then go to college. I figured I'd be drafted later, and I was.

My original dream was to become an engineer, which seemed natural because I loved to build things and was good at math—or so I thought. I had A's in math in high school, but I took an advanced math class as a freshman at La Crosse State University (now the University of Wisconsin-La Crosse) in 1946. I was in the wrong class and failed it, which ended my engineering dream. I was so discouraged that I dropped out of college.

Melvin Hickenbothum, back row left, is shown with the early royalty of the La Crescent Apple Festival. Shown in back row with him are Lois Lintelman, Apple Festival Queen Donna Lintelman, and Jackie Jones. Middle row, from left are Mary Lou Kuehn, Joane Benson, Elaine Moore, and Zeta Oldenburg. In front row are Virginia Gittens and Lenora Beach. La Crescent Area Historical Society.

Chapter 4

Uncle Sam Wanted Me

Dropping out of school meant I lost my student defer-ment, leading to my being drafted into the Army in 1950. I had a fourteen-week basic training course at Fort Riley, Kansas. During that time there were no instructors or cadre on the base. Our commander selected me to become a mortar instructor. I was briefly trained and then proceeded to teach all of the new recruits about this weapon. We became very proficient on firing the mortar shell at a target 500 yards away.

A mortar, which resembles a small canon, is three-foot high and four-inches in diameter. The operator drops the shell down a tube and when it hits the bottom, it is ignited and propelled forward. The mortar crew adjusted the mortar for wind velocity and elevation to reach its target.

During basic training, I had a little side business, sewing on patches, insignias, buttons, and stripes to indicate rank on the recruits' shirts and jackets. I sent home the money I earned to be deposited in our local bank.

I made money in other ways, including loaning my buddies money—at double interest—when they ran out of funds after blowing their pay on poker and craps. Their loans had to be repaid by the next payday. I always had extra money because playing chess with my friend from another camp, Werner Schroeder, was my entertainment in those days.

I did go out with the guys some. One night a friend with a new Buick took five of us into Junction City, Kansas, where we searched for dance halls. I sat drinking our favorite beverage—beer—to gain enough false courage to ask a young woman to dance. One in our group began dancing with a lady, only to find himself suddenly surrounded by six guys.

"Do you realize you're dancing with my wife?" "So what?" he responded.

"Do you want to make something of it? Let's take this outside."

As we left the dance hall, each group got into a car. We followed them up a block and stopped. The men in the other car jumped out with brass knuckles and chains. I pretended to be too drunk to get out of the car, sitting in the back seat while my friends called me "yellow."

With those brass knuckles and chains used by the other guys, our men were pummeled into a bloody mess.

They crawled back to the car with bloodied noses, eye injuries, broken arms and legs, and concussions. After seeing what happened to my friends, I knew I had been smart to not get out of that car. I had no desire to get involved in the biggest, most brutal, and worthless fight I had ever seen.

Near the end of my basic training, the sharpest soldier I knew appeared one day to talk to all of us about the 11th Airborne. If we chose to become paratroopers, we could receive more training and get an extra seventy-five dollars in monthly compensation for hazardous duty.

I volunteered to become a paratrooper for the 11th Airborne,

A unit that dated back to World War I, although it did not see actual action in that war. The 11th arrived in Liverpool, England, on November 8, 1918, three days before the Armistice. In 1943, the 11th was reactivated after the U.S. Army observed how efficient large-scale airborne formations were for the Germans. A history of the division described the training as arduous: [12]

There were 250 foot (76 meter) and 34 foot (10 meter) towers that were built from which prospective airborne troops would jump off of to simulate landing by parachute. They had lengthy forced marches and practice jumps from transport aircraft; to pause in the doorway of an aircraft during a practice jump resulted in an automatic failure for the candidate. The resultant failure rate was accordingly high, but there was never a shortage of candidates, especially for the American divisions, as the rate of pay was much higher than that of an ordinary infantryman. The 11th Division was part of many key battles late in World War II, particularly the invasion of the Philippines. After the war ended, the 11th was part of the occupying force in Japan until 1949. In 1950, the division participated in a large-scale training exercise designed to perfect resupplying techniques in the field, techniques later used in Korea.[13]

When I joined the 11th, I had no idea that Dick Kathan, a childhood friend, also had volunteered, from another camp. Divine providence put us both in the same division, the same company, the same barracks, and even the same bunk beds at Fort Campbell, Kentucky. I lost the flip of the coin, which meant I had the top bunk. It was a good thing I wasn't a bed wetter.

Landing off of the top bunk was nothing like jumping out of an airplane as a paratrooper. The airborne training was intense, beginning with jumping from a 34-foot tower, hooked onto a cable that ran down to a sand pit on the ground. Since we would land at thirty-five miles per hour, technique was everything. We landed on our toes, then our heels and calves before rolling on to our hip and our push up muscle under our arms. This procedure is called the (PLF) or Parachute Landing Form.

Our trainers insisted that we keep our hands down and that our hands are in front of our reserve chute when we jumped. If we did not, the ropes from the back chute could get entangled in our helmets, literally tearing off our heads. You have to get your hands exactly right if you want to live to tell the story of your jump.

To impress anyone who fails to do this critical technique properly, the sergeant ordered any transgressor to walk fifty times around the training area with hands stretched out flapping like wings while repeating, "I'm a big-ass bird." I know this because they made me do it—once!

The chutes we had were difficult to control for speed, direction, and oscillation (swinging back and forth). One man died when he landed on a hospital lightening rod.

Redesigned chutes today allow paratroopers to guide where they are going like an airplane wing and make a much softer landing at two to four miles per hour.

"Our airborne troops using the T-11 Parachute are equipped with a system that provides superior safety and reliability while improving mission readiness," BAE Systems' Individual Protection Systems Director of Warfighter Equipment Programs, Greg Kraak, commented in a company press release issued at the start of March 2011. "The improved harness system and slower rate of descent reduces the risk of injury, and the redesigned canopy provides the advantage of carrying more combat equipment."[14]

It was only after we had jumped many times from the towers (parachute landing forms or PLF) and had perfected the technique that we jumped from an airplane at 1,000 feet. It is human nature not to want to do this, a reason that we practiced many times.

On each plane there were 40 men, 20 men on each side. Each paratrooper held a static line hook in his hands to snap on to the airplane cable. This pulled an O-ring out of the parachute after leaving the door so the chute opened at the right time. We were told to keep our head down after leaving the static line so it didn't rip our heads off. It was serious business. Men were hurt and even killed in these practice jumps.

By the time we were on that plane, we were like sheep, following one after another when the jumpmaster yelled "Go!" As we shuffled to the door, we placed our hands on the outside of the fuselage. As we jumped into space, the wind hit us at 120 miles per hour. We went from 120 mph to 0 mph in three seconds in the opening shock.

To have the confidence to do this crazy thing of jumping out of an airplane, we reminded ourselves that many others had done it safely before us. We did not dwell on those who were injured or died.

To get our airborne paratrooper wings, we had to do five jumps in a single day and march twenty-five miles. We became desensitized to the height and danger, but were exhausted by the end of that incredible day.

I served in the Korean conflict era and had expected to be part of the Battle of Inchon in September, 1950. During our early days at Fort Campbell, we were trained for Inchon. The entire division was on our jump planes—C82s, C19s, and DC3s—dressed in combat gear for many hours waiting in the tarmac. Beads of sweat ran down our faces, and fear strained our bodies.

After what seemed like forever, the pilot came back of the plane and said, "Guys we've got great news. The 11th Division was called off for the Inchon invasion." We learned that another airborne division jumped Inchon with 98 percent casualties. Instead, we became a defensive unit within the United States.

(Jack) as a paratrooper ready to board DC3 for a jump in the
U.S. Army.

(Jack) as a paratrooper in my dress uniform. Once I
dropped out of college, Uncle Sam drafted me.

The Lord Saved Me Again.

During our stay at Fort Campbell, our division was ordered to Camp Drum, New York, for winter training. We boarded our aircraft to make a winter assault on the camp. We were to be the second wave to jump from about 1,000 feet above ground.

Quickly a problem developed with the new steel backpacks attached to the front of our reserve chutes. As the first wave jumped the drop zone (DZ), their steel backpacks let loose from the harnesses, flew up and hit them in their faces. Many men were killed.

Just as we approached the drop zone, we were called off due to the fatalities in the first wave.

The Lord Saved Me Again.

Forty men on the plane with what is called the twenty-men stick on each side—getting ready to jump out of the plane. I can't identify myself in that photo, but generally I was the first man to jump. U.S. Army Photo.

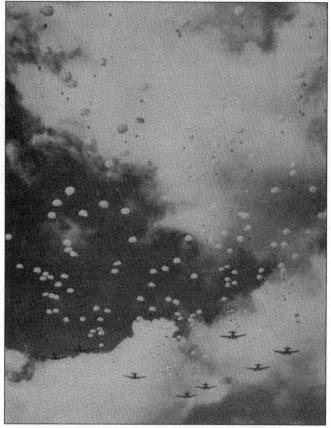

This photo shows a mass jump of 11th Airborne.
U.S. Army photo.

Hokah Accident

One month before I was to be discharged from the Army, I came home on a three-day pass, which ended on Saturday night. Sunday was to be a day of grace—I did not have to report back that day, but I certainly had to be there in time for Monday morning duty.

I borrowed my dad's new Jeep station wagon to visit my girlfriend in Caledonia, Minnesota, about a half hour from La Crescent. Returning from my date, I fell asleep just before I had to navigate a sharp ninety-degree downhill turn into Hokah, Minnesota, about three miles from La Crescent. I rolled eight times down an embankment, crashing through a chicken coop. The top of the car was reduced from six feet to three feet, and I flew through the windshield. Broken glass was everywhere, and I was bleeding profusely from my head wounds.

A neighbor heard the accident, rushed over, and pulled me feet first out of the rear of the wreckage. He wrapped my bleeding head in an old blanket and rushed me to Grandview Hospital in La Crosse.

I required surgery—sixty stitches—and after a few days at Grandview I was then transferred to the Army Hospital at Fort McCoy, Wisconsin, about forty miles from La Crescent. Because I was supposed to be back at Fort Campbell, I was listed as AWOL—Away without Leave. A guard stood by my hospital door the three weeks I recuperated. An MP was to take me back to Fort Campbell—650 miles—under armed guard, despite my being a top-caliber soldier.

Since I didn't want that armed guard escort, I called a friend in La Crescent to secretly pick me up and take me to the railroad station in Tomah, Wisconsin, so I could travel back to Fort Campbell on my own. The guard was still outside my door when my friend arrived. I jumped out of my hospital room window and got into his car between the back and front seats with my Duffel bag covering me. At the front gate of Camp McCoy, a guard looked in and told us we could be on our way. My friend then dropped me off at the train station, and I headed south.

When I arrived at Fort Campbell, guards checked my ID and were surprised that I returned to the fort without armed guards. When they realized I came back on my own, they said I had true integrity. There was no way that I would have done anything but return to duty. I registered back into my barracks and reported to my senior officer to tell him about the accident. He accepted my explanation.

I was soon honorably discharged and even better; my first sergeant successfully pleaded my case to have all of the medical expenses back in Wisconsin paid for as service connected. I thought this was the Lord's way of allowing me to live!

The Lord Saved Me Again!

The accident was covered in the *Hokah Chief* newspaper with the headline, "Car—Chicken Coop—Soldier Hurt!"

This was not the only time that I was recognized in the *Hokah Chief.* It was so unusual to have two local soldiers—Dick Kathan and me—in the same unit that the newspaper, published an article about our experience on April 23, 1953. "When you stand at the edge of that open door and look out at nothing but thin air and see the face of the earth thousands of feet below you, 'It's against human nature to jump into space,'" one of us said. The newspaper didn't specify which one of us made that comment. But we did jump, even though you wanted to say "no" when the jumpmaster said, "go" and tapped you on your legs as you stood at the door of the plane. We hit the ground at 35 mph. We knew we needed to be relaxed and not stiff legged or we could be crippled for life when we landed.

On one jump, a paratrooper was so close to me that he landed on my chute—I had to jerk my lines to get out of his way so we did not hit each other, which would have killed us both. Another time, I saw another man nearly fall to the earth before his chute opened. When he landed safely, he announced, "I made it," and then dropped over and died from a heart attack.

I came out of the Army more disciplined than when I went in and ready to go back to college and complete my degree. I was more focused and this time my grades could not go any higher. My degree was in political science, sociology, geography, and meteorology. I did so well that professors asked me to teach some classes. My sister Cynthia and I had the honor of graduating together in 1955 from La Crosse State University.

Notes

12 http://www.11thairbornedivision.com/h o m e/ camp-mackall

13 http://www.usmilitariaforum.com/forums/lofiversion/ index.php/t106.html

14 "New T-11 Parachutes for U.S. Army Paratroopers," Armed Forces International News, March 2011, http://www. armedforces-int.com/news/new-t-11-parachutes-for-us-armyparatroopers.html

Having two local boys (Jack Welch and Dick Kathan) in the same unit was reason enough for the newspaper to publish a story about us. As the headline said, it was against human nature to jump out of an airplane.

Chapter 5

Building Our Own Business

My first job after graduating from college in 1955 was at the Trane Company, Laboratory a pioneering air conditioning manufacturer once on the Fortune 500 list. Our job was to improve the efficiency of centrifugal fans.

I was paid very well for this boring job as a second assistant/Pitot tube operator. I held the tube all day at a wind tunnel, where others measured the wind velocity of the fans and the static pressure of the wind against the tunnel itself.

After I was there about nine months, I figured there had to be a better way to do this test. I had an idea and drew it up in a plan. The director of the Trane Lab gave me authority to build the automatic Pitot tube machine, which I knew might put me out of the best paying job I'd ever had.

My machine worked—it automatically recorded the wind velocity and static pressure in different increments.

My team leader took the credit for it, a good lesson for me that people will take your ideas to better themselves. It's happened to me all of my life.

Dad must have sensed my unhappiness with having lost the credit for developing the automatic Pitot tube machines. Or, he may have had this idea about going into business with me. Either way, one day he said to me, "Jump in the car. I want to drive you downtown to show you something."

We stopped at First and Sycamore Streets in La Crescent, an area below the highway that once had been the site of the train depot where my parents met. By 1955, it was more of an industrial area, including a fifty-foot by 125-foot lot, which he showed me.

"This is where we will build a lumberyard," he announced, totally surprising me.

This was the first I had heard of this business, and I instantly saw three problems. This lot was too small for a lumberyard. We didn't know anything about the lumber business, and we had no start-up money.

"Dad, how are we going to do this?"

"We're going to do it by faith."

Dad reached out his hand to shake mine.

"A handshake is a bond of integrity," Dad told me. "No matter what you have stated on paper, it does not touch the worth of a man's honesty and integrity like a handshake."

When my dad showed me that small lot in La Crescent and told me his dream, I was excited. I quit my job at Trane as he suggested.

I wasn't afraid of the unknown as many people are, preventing them from recognizing and using their God-given gifts. My dad sensed the gifts and abilities I had that could be used in our business and personal life. With no money, equipment, or facilities—and with little knowledge of the lumber business—my mind raced constantly about how we would get the lumberyard going.

This tiny lot was the first home for Consolidated Builders Supply Later CBS Homes.

We started Consolidated Builders Supply (CBS) without money or anyone in the area knowing about our start-up, but we had an inner drive to succeed.

On this small, barren lot we constructed an office and small warehouse. Dad and his good friend, Rome Baker, took our pick up one day to drum up new business. Within minutes, Dad called with a report that there had been a mishap.

"Jack, you will never believe what happened," he said. "We were heading south on Oak Street when we suddenly saw a young woman mowing her lawn in a bikini."

They were so fixated on watching the young woman that they drove over the homeowner's mailbox. Dad asked me to bring a new 4 by 4 post and a mailbox "pronto."

"Looking at that gal was worth ten mailboxes and posts," he told me.

His friend, who had only one eye, added, "Ralph, I wish I had two eyes to look at that view!"

To start this business, we needed someone to take a chance buying building materials from us. I drove my pickup truck all over La Crescent, looking for a home to supply. I came upon Mike Kletzke, who was digging footing for his new home. After talking with Mike, he agreed to consider a bid from us. He gave us his house plan so we could estimate the lumber.

Bill Wiedman, a friend of my dad's, ran a lumberyard in a nearby town. I sat down with Bill over three weeks while Bill taught me how to develop a lumber material list from a house plan. Bill took the time—without pay— to methodically teach me about building a proper home, including lumber markups and estimating. I absorbed the knowledge like a sponge.

I called twenty-three lumberyards within our area for pricing our lumber list for Mike's house. I took the average and presented it as a bid along with a lumber list. "The price looks good. You've got the job," Mike said. I gave him a two percent discount for payment upon delivery of the materials. With no lumber in our lumberyard, I searched newspapers for lumber discounts. I found a new start-up cash-and-carry lumberyard about seventy-five miles from La Crescent. They sold lumber at their cost to get people into their business.

I drove our one-and-a-half-ton truck and picked up the mountainous load of Mike's lumber. I wrote a check to pay for the lumber with no money in our bank, something we could never do today. On the way home, I stopped to take off the "Cash and Carry" sign stapled to the lumber and replaced it with our Consolidated Builders Supply sign.

We had so much weight on the truck that the front wheels bobbled off the ground as I continued home. The next morning, I delivered the load to Mike, who was pleased with the quality of the lumber and that it was reversed loaded so what he needed first was on top. He gave me a check, which I deposited in the bank to cover the check I wrote the previous day.

Our first truck, which we used on that first job as Consolidated Builders Supply. It was so weighed down, I have no idea how I got it back to La Crescent. Our minds were equally weighed down with worry about getting the money in the bank before the yard cashed my check. All worked out well.

Armed with a measuring tape at night, I continued to visit job sites to learn how houses went together. I measured hallways, doorways, and windows, all to gain knowledge that would help me estimate houses.

For the first year and a half, Dad and I worked day and night but did not receive a check for all of our efforts—everything we had went back into the business to buy building materials and eventually to add workers. I barely knew what a two by four was when we started. I grew up on a fruit farm—not in construction, although I had made those houses as a kid, possibly because of that innate mechanical ability that I call a gift. As a young man in an even younger business, I knew I had to be careful and methodical in my daily tasks to make it a success. However, I had an entrepreneurial spirit that drove me to accomplish the tasks that were laid before me.

I quickly learned these tips:

Be organized in my daily tasks. My mind constantly raced with ideas about how to start the business without any money, facilities, equipment, or knowledge of the lumber business. We were not known for the field we entered.

Be creative. Many people who start businesses fail because they do not appreciate all that a new company needs to be successful. It's not just about dollars and cents and a good product. I learned to think creatively and ask questions of those who were willing and able to answer them, filtering out advice that may not be practical or apply to my business. I knew I always wanted to have a solid relationship with these people so they would be willing to answer future questions that arise.

Be a people person. I had to be the kind of person who people are drawn to and want to help. Courtesy, graciousness, and thanking others for the help I received were critical qualities—things we should do in business and our personal lives. I needed the humility to ask others to share their knowledge with me. I then gleaned from information that I needed for my business.

Multi-task. I needed to learn and manage many elements in our business at the same time, including:

- Hiring an accountant who would help create profit and loss (P &L) statements from the first day.
- Finding the best sources for buying lumber and millwork wholesale.
- Transporting lumber from the wholesaler to our lumberyard and building sites.
- Building and selling houses. Many nights I designed and estimated house plans in our office and at home. I did not have previous design experience. I had one year of mechanical design in high school, but none in college.
- Marking up product to allow for profit while still being marketable to contractors.
- Equipment we needed to get started, particularly until we could afford a forklift. We started with a one-and-a-half-ton truck to

move product by hand. We built a curved sales counter and added a triple invoice machine for contractor billing.

Have integrity. When Dad and I started the lumber business we shook hands to seal the partnership. My dad said no matter what you write in a contract, it still can be beaten. "But a handshake is a bond between one man to another," he said. "This shows integrity. Integrity is a sound, moral principle with uprightness, honesty, and sincerity."

The days when a business can be run on just a hand-shake may have passed, but integrity is still critical in your business and personal life. The people with whom you work and live must know that you are a person of integrity and that you have the same expectation for them. Integrity means honesty, sincerity, and moral uprightness.

Nourish an inventive spirit. As the lumberyard grew, builders called us for advice on projects, along with estimates for the materials they would need. I gave them counsel on their questions on how something would look when it was finished or made suggestions about what they should do in a certain area of their plan. I may not have been formally trained in building and design, but the Lord gave me the gift of picturing a finished project in my mind before it was designed or completed.

I also had a good eye for color coordination, also very helpful in building houses.

Unsinkable Business

We had done so well as Consolidated Builders Supply that for a time we thought we were unsinkable as a business. Willing to build whatever people wanted, we took on a project for Joe Strupp—the same man who dynamited our septic system—to build him a 16-by-5-by-2-ft. high scow boat to be made out of fir flooring.

Our early CBS Homes offices in La Crescent.

I developed a steamer that allowed us to bend the flooring for the bow so it curved down to the bottom of the boat. When it was done in a couple weeks, I called Joe to tell him it was ready.

He was so pleased with how it looked that he put me in the same category as Noah.

That, of course, was before we put the boat in the water, loaded down with dredging material, including cables, ropes, pulleys, and wenches plus a forty-horse-power motor on the back of the boat. We pushed him off from shore, and he started the motor.

All of a sudden we saw water pouring in from every direction on the boat, and Joe working feverishly to bail out. I still have this image of Joe waist high in the water going down in this pond that he had dredged to about fifty-feet deep. The last thing that I saw was Joe's middle finger extending out of the water as he and the boat went down.

We knew he would be fine, but Dad suggested we get out of there quickly so he didn't kill us. What we learned from that experience was to stay out of the boat-building business.

That was not the only unusual project that we had. Farmers came into our business and wanted to know if we could build a round-roof building. Immediately, I designed and developed a system that sawed the lumber into a curve, which allowed us to build a round-roof structure. We then expanded into pole barns and dairy barns, building the largest dairy farm in the La Crosse area. Our building crews worked on sites in Minnesota, Iowa, and Wisconsin.

Then there was the client in Coon Valley, Wisconsin, in the 1960s, who wanted us to build him a complete nuclear bomb shelter. After World War II, Americans were in tremendous fear of the Russians and the hydrogen bomb. Civil Defense authorities even recommended basement or buried backyard shelters for protection in a nuclear war.

My customer didn't care how much it cost—he was determined to have a complete concrete underground bunker for his family. The walls were one-foot thick and the top of the underground shelter was two-and-a-half feet thick concrete. Inside my customer's shelter were shelves for food and water.

As frightened as we all were, most of the people I knew realized we would not want to survive a nuclear war if it meant living in an underground shelter for years. What would we come up to find? Could there be enough food and supplies with us underground to last as long as it would take for the fallout to disperse? And what would we do down there? It would be way too much togetherness for most families to be together like that for months or even years.

Chapter 6

Meeting Jann

Consolidated Builders Supply had been going for a couple years when a friend in La Crescent, Jackie Jones, told me the St. Francis Hospital School of Nursing in La Crosse was going to have a dance on Saturday. She wondered if I would bring a few friends to dance with the sixty girls in the class. That was an offer I could not refuse.

Women went crazy for my dad's 1953 Studebaker Starlight Commander Coupé, which had a candy-apple body with a cream-colored top. That sports car, a real beauty, could go 140 miles an hour; I knew that because I used to take the guys in it to Rochester, Minnesota, to hear the big bands—including Count Basie, Benny Goodman, and Glen Miller.

Naturally, I borrowed the Starlight for that dance. I was with Sally Walsh, a very nice woman, but my eyes were on her best friend, Jann Deen Witt, who was with my best friend, Bruce Nelson. After the dance, the four of us got something to eat in La Crosse.

The "1953" Studebaker Starlight Commander Coupe, in which I picked up Jann for our first date. Like her, this car was a real beauty

Jann Deen Witt was one of the nursing students I met at a dance at St. Francis Nursing School.

Jann and I did not connect again for three years. There was no communication and no dating. I thought of Jann during that time but never took action. Then one night at about two o'clock in the morning, I had enough false courage—alcohol— in me to finally call her. I had been in a downtown La Crosse nightclub, which was closing at bar time. After the lights went out, I was feeling lonely, so I thought I'd call that woman who impressed me three years before.

"I've been sitting here thinking of you and was wondering if it was possible to get together," I told her.

"No way," she said. "Not at this hour."

Bang! She hung up, clearly and rightfully disgusted with me.

The next day I tried her again, calling at a reasonable hour. She said she was busy—going waterskiing with a friend. I was turned down twice. I felt like a bed sheet. Finally, in desperation I called her again, asking if she was interested in going to the Interstate Fair in La Crosse. She agreed.

As Jann said, "I think Jack was not used to having girls turn him down. That made me a little more intriguing to him."

Jann told me later that each time she said no to me, she was hoping I would call back. I had impressed her back then, too. We both saw each other as someone very special.

"I thought he was my prince in shining armor," Jann said. "But three years went by before he called me for a date."

As it turned out, she was about to become engaged to another man. As I was not a Christian at the time; only the Lord could have put us together. I remember everything about our first date, including what she wore: a beige blouse, rust colored slacks, and saddle shoes.

Jann and I were very happy in 1957.

I asked Bruce if he minded if I dated her as he was with her at that dance three years earlier. He did not; he already was seeing Mary Martha "Marti" Swenson, whom he married in 1957.

I was relieved. For me, it was love at first sight, even if it took me three years to realize Jann was the love of my life. From there, we started dating three or four times a week. After six months, I talked to her parents, Dale and Lois Witt, about marrying her. Dale's biggest concern was whether I could provide a good living for his daughter. When I promised I would, he agreed.

That Christmas 1957, I got down on my knees and asked her to marry me. She agreed, asking only why it took me that long. She saw me as someone coming from the same faith as she did, Presbyterian, which she felt meant we shared the same values.

Six months later, Jann and I married on June 21, 1958, seven days before my thirtieth birthday. Jann wore the beautiful wedding dress that my sister Cynthia wore ten months earlier in her wedding to Earl Good. Cynthia offered that dress to Jann, who called it a "wonderful gesture of love. I tried on her dress and it fit perfectly so I wore it for our wedding, feeling so honored."

The ceremony was in the First Presbyterian Church in La Crosse, since our Presbyterian Church in La Crescent was too small. The ceremony was held in the late afternoon followed by a reception in the Cargill House, a "massive house" built by William W. Cargill after he established his commodity business in the city.[15] The Cargill house was a beautiful place with gold leaf ceiling. I can't imagine why such a beautiful house was torn down.

The La Crosse Tribune described the house as one of the city's eight biggest losses in historic houses in an article in 2007 that addressed houses and buildings at risk. "Though associated with the grain business, the Cargill's were local philanthropists. Their grand mansion was built in 1881–1883 at the northeast corner of Cass Street and West Avenue and extensively remodeled in 1896 to about 1906 by Ellen Cargill. The Cargill estate gifted the house to First Presbyterian Church in 1927. The church maintained the house until maintenance costs prohibited continued use. It was razed in 1975, after local preservationists listed it on the National Register of Historic Places. Today, only the fence remains in front of the new addition to First Presbyterian Church."[16]

It was a wonderful ceremony and reception but around 8:30 or 9:00 p.m. I felt we had to get out of there to start our honeymoon. We hopped into my 1957 Ford Fairlane, a green two-toned car with a white top. We had no specific plans, except heading north. Uncle Gerald Welch slipped me twenty dollars in the reception line, and that was the money we used for our entire honeymoon.

Immediately after starting our drive, we were hit with the most awful stench you could imagine. I stopped the car and discovered our "friends" had not stopped at tying cans and shoes to the back bumper with a "just married sign," a common practice in those days. They put Limburger cheese, considered one of the smelliest cheeses in the world, on the muffler. It was so terrible and long lasting that I eventually had to sell that car.

I had other things on my mind that night, however, and spotted a hotel in Dresbach, just a few miles up the road from La Crescent. "I can't hold the wheel," I told Jann. "I'm going right into the motel." We soon discovered our friends and family were not finished with their teasing. Jann's cousins had gotten into her suitcase and sewn her nightgown shut so she could not get into it.

We continued on to Brainerd, Minnesota, where we found a cabin at, "Its It Resort". About the second or third day, the owner knocked on our door to make sure we were OK. She gave us a box of strawberries that were just in season.

During the day we fished and entertained ourselves at night. One night we went to a dance in Brainerd, where a guy tried to take Jann from me, which caused a little ruckus. I won.

All told, our week-long honeymoon cost about twenty dollars—the money my uncle slipped me at the reception. I was so grateful because at that time, I didn't have two dollars to my name. That twenty dollars was enough to get us to Brainerd—about 200 miles north in lake country at twenty-five cents a gallon for gas and for our food and motels.

Our wedding day on June 21, 1958, at the First Presbyterian Church in La Crosse.

My wonderful sister Cynthia was the first to wear this beautiful dress when she married Earl Good in 1957. Jann was honored that her new sister in law shared it with her. Twenty-five years later, our daughter Kendra wore this dress at her wedding to Jon Sopher.

Our honeymoon cabin in Brainerd with the smelly 1957 Ford Fairlane parked in front.

More about Jann

Jann Deen Witt was born at home in La Crosse to Lois Grace (Nimocks) and Dale Francis Witt. As the story was told, Dr. Archie Skemp—the premiere deliverer of babies in those days—came to their home when Lois was in labor. He slept on a davenport by the stove until she was ready to deliver. Her mother then stayed in bed for a week, which was the tradition then.

"I know the exact bedroom where I was born because Aunt Sarah Jane lived there until she died. I also spent many hours playing with my cousins on North 11th Street in that house," she said.

Although she was born in La Crosse, Jann grew up on a dairy farm in southeastern Minnesota as the oldest of a family of two boys and two girls. Without television, the kids created their own games indoors and outdoors. The girls helped with the garden, house, and yard, while the boys milked and did other outside work with their dad.

In the 1930s, decided differences existed between rural and urban areas of Minnesota. The Witt farm was like others in rural Minnesota. It had no electricity until it came in the 1930s via the Rural Electrification Administration (REA). Prior to the REA's creation in 1935, ninety percent of urban areas had electricity, but only ten percent nationally in rural areas—thirteen percent in

Minnesota. By 1939 in Minnesota, thirty percent of rural areas had electricity.[17]

"REA came in and installed poles and lines for electricity when I was nine years old," Jann remembered. "What a thrill! There were no more kerosene or Aladdin lamps to read by. It made such a tremendous difference."

The Witt's did not have a furnace but had an oil heater in the living/dining room. Heat rose through a floor register to heat the upstairs. They had a cozy wood stove in the kitchen, which heated water for baths and dishes.

"As a family, we always had our meals around the kitchen table after we said a prayer of thanks," Jann said.

A teakettle was constantly on the wood stove in the kitchen, which also had a ten-gallon side-mounted water reservoir that provided steam—natural humidity—for the house. Saturday night was reserved for baths—as it was in my home and most rural houses. Jann's mother turned on the oven and opened the oven door so there would be warmth when they took their baths in the large round metal washtub in front of the oven.

Jann and sister Jill went first, followed by the boys—Lynn and Frank—after they came in from the barn after chores. They all shared the same bath water except for additional hot water, added as needed. Between Saturdays, they took sponge baths in the morning before heading off to school.

The Witt farm had an outhouse that the family used in all weather, including winter. The family had running water only in the barn when the Witt's moved to their farm in 1951.

"My dad dug a seven-foot-deep trench by hand from the barn to the house so we could have running water," Jann recalled. "Wow! What an improvement when the job was done."

The bathroom was added to the house in 1958, shortly before our wedding. I was proud to draw the plans for the bathroom.

On Sundays, Jann's mom put dinner in the oven to cook while she and the four kids went to the Presbyterian Church, about fifteen miles away. By the time they returned, their father was done with chores, and they enjoyed that meal. "How I thank the Lord for such a wonderful mother—she was like the woman portrayed in Proverbs 31:10–-31," Jann said.

A wife of noble character who can find? She is worth far more than rubies.

Her husband has full confidence in her and lacks nothing of value.
She brings him good, not harm, all the days of her life. ...
She sets about her work vigorously; her arms are strong for her tasks. ...

She is clothed with strength and dignity; she can laugh at the days to come.

She speaks with wisdom and faithful instruction is on her tongue.

She watches over the affairs of her household and does not eat the bread of idleness.

Her children arise and call her blessed; her husband also, and he praises her ...

Charm is deceptive, and beauty is fleeting; but a woman who fears the LORD is to be praised.

Honor her for all that her hands have done and let her works bring her praise at the city gate. **(NIV)**[18]

Jann's parents, Dale and Lois Witt.

Jann tells other stories of life on the farm, including the annual arrival of Santa Claus on Christmas Eve. In her family, he put up and decorated the tree during the night, leaving presents to be discovered by the children.

"The next morning, we would come down and see the tree decorated. What a thrill that was!" she recalled.

Aunts, uncles, and cousins came on Christmas Day to celebrate together. "Our farm was a place where so many loved ones and friends came to visit often," Jann said.

Jann and her siblings attended a one-room schoolhouse that served the fifteen children from first through eighth grade—no kindergarten. A major event each Friday afternoon was an all-student spelling bee. "I always enjoyed it and learned to love spelling and English," Jann said.

After the school closed, they were bused to Caledonia, Minnesota. After a year and a half in school there, Jann's father bought a farm near Sheldon, Minnesota. Moving in March of her freshman year of high school, Jann was devastated to leave her friends at Caledonia High School. She made friends at Houston High School, from which she graduated in 1954.

Jann's mother had always wanted to be a nurse but could not go to school. After her father died suddenly, she had to work to support her brother in college, a common practice then. Lois became a telephone operator in La Crosse.

After graduation, Jann went to St. Francis School of Nursing, fulfilling her mother's dream. After studying for three years and working at St. Francis, Jann graduated in 1958.

When we returned to La Crescent after our honeymoon, we moved into our apartment on the second floor of a house across the street from Crucifixion Church. Jann earned $300 a month as a nurse at Gundersen Clinic, which was big money in those days. Our rent was $45 a month, but there still were many times when we didn't have enough money to go around. This was a time when Dad and I were not taking a salary from the business.

Notes

15 W.W. Cargill, http://www.wisconsinstories.org/lacrosse/essay/index.cfm?page=9

16 Geri Parlin, "Are these structures worth saving?" *La Crosse Tribune,* August 26, 2007.

17 http://stories.mnhs.org/stories/mgg/resources/glossary.

18 http://www.biblegateway.com/passage/?search=Proverbs+31%3A10-31&version=NIV

From the left: (Jack), Jann my wife, Cynthia and her husband Earl Good. 1959 photo.

Chapter 7

Our Family

Like so many young couples, Jann and I longed for a family. We were thrilled when our first child, Kendra Deen, was born on January 21, 1960.

Brent John followed on May 22, 1962. "What a transition having two babies," Jann said. "Our arms were always full holding one or the other of our precious little ones."

In 1967, we welcomed our third child, James Allen, who was born just five minutes after midnight on February 15. "We still considered him our Valentine," Jann likes to say. I agree.

We built a CBS Home for ourselves in 1969, and it remains our family home. When we built our home, it was located in the country but had the benefits of city water and sewer .

Each of our children is unique, different, loving, and a gift from God. At meals we all laughed as they made faces at each other and told jokes and stories about their day. When they were little, they were always busy learning to help with household chores while music played in the background. At night we had story time, and the children said their bedtime prayers.

Jann and I took turns posing with the kids on our way to church: James in front, with Brent behind him and Kendra. Photos circa 1970.

Jack and the kids.

Kendra

Among the memories of Kendra was the night she and two friends went cruising in our new Lincoln Town Car. The next day I wondered why the car transmission did not work. With tears in her eyes, Kendra confessed to doing what she called a "neutral drop." One of her friends told Kendra to rev up the engine to 3000 rpm, slam the shift into drive, and then into reverse. The result was a need for a new transmission in our new car. "Dad, I won't do it again," she promised many times. Kendra worked hard in everything she did, including band, choir, cheerleading, the school newspaper, and gymnastics in high school. I built her a balance beam in the basement, which allowed her to practice gymnastics, in which she excelled.

After high school graduation, Kendra attended Northwestern Bible College where she met her future husband, Jon Sopher. Kendra transferred to the University of Wisconsin-La Crosse and graduated with a degree in elementary school teaching. She was a wonderful teacher and taught second grade for a number of years.

When she married Jon Sopher in the Bethany Evangelical Free Church in La Crosse, she wanted to wear the wedding dress that her mother and Aunt Cynthia wore. She looked beautiful in that dress. She and Jon have four beautiful children—Bergen, Kyleigh, Natalie, and Andrew.

Our first two children, Brent, left, and Kendra.

Kendra looked as beautiful as her mother and
aunt in this wedding dress.

Brent

Our second child, Brent, has many gifts, including music. After seeing me regularly play the set of drums I received as a gift one Christmas, Brent decided he wanted drum lessons. Soon Brent and his musical buddies jammed regularly in our basement. They formed a group that played professionally while in college.

During high school, Brent played football and was point guard in basketball. While carrying the football as a running back, he must have felt invincible until he and a defender hit head on. When both boys were carried off the field, we parents on the sideline felt our pounding hearts bursting in our chests. We could easily have had heart attacks until we learned there were no serious injuries.

Brent was artistic, entering many pictures he painted in a church youth competition. His interest reflected his early acceptance of Christ and heart for the Lord. Brent graduated from the University of Wisconsin-La Crosse and then earned a certificate in Bible studies at a Torchbearers Bible School in England—the Capernwray Bible School in Carnforth, Lancashire, England. He used his studies in finance as the foundation for his retirement planning business, Welshire Capital, in Onalaska, Wisconsin, just north of La Crosse.

After thirty years in business, Welshire Capital has grown to serve clients in fourteen states. Brent and the Welshire team help clients retire in confidence. Brent is an author, columnist, and frequent radio show guest. He has served on many national boards related to his business.

He and his wife Marianne (Waitrovich) have three beautiful children—Jacob, Ryan, and Jessica.

Brent in front of a much-loved tree in our yard.

James

Born five years after his brother Brent, James's interests as a child included trick riding his bicycle and skateboarding. He and his friends made a slingshot out of a rubber tube and a baseball glove that they used to launch water balloons two to three blocks away. During high school, he took the skills he gained playing basketball on our hoop to La Crescent High School, where he was a point guard.

James, who also had mechanical skills, wanted me to help him build a motorcycle. While looking through the newspaper, we found a three-wheeled frame that included the three wheels and balloon tires.

After the purchase, we located a twin cylinder 18 HP motorcycle engine. We geared down the motor and found a seat supplier. After painting the machine a brilliant red, our family took it out for a time trial. After we got the three-wheeler up to 80 mph in second gear, we didn't have the nerve to shift it into high gear.

After graduating from the University of Wisconsin-Madison in organic farming and horticulture, James bought a 180-acre farm in Reedsburg, Wisconsin. His farm, Avalanche Organics, was well known in the Midwest for his advanced organic farming methods. Avalanche Organics described itself as a "premiere organic/biodynamic specialty vegetable, fruit, and herb farm located in the beautiful Driftless Area of southwest Wisconsin, along the fertile banks of the Kickapoo River."

James met his wife Kristin Karrer while they attended the University of Wisconsin-Madison. They have two beautiful children, Neona and Nathaniel.

On their farm, they grew 175 varieties of fruits, vegetables, and herbs that served community-supported agriculture, the Dane County Farmer's Market, natural food stores, and upscale restaurants in Madison, Chicago, Milwaukee, and Minneapolis. They loved the work but found farming left them with little time to enjoy their family, so they moved to Grass Valley, California, about fifty miles east of Sacramento. James makes his living in a variety of ways, including landscaping, fencing, driveway work, and building greenhouses.

James and Kristen purchased a business in California that is the largest seller of organic clothing west of the Mississippi.

The Sixth Member of Our Family—Duke

James had a golden retriever named Duke who got in trouble so much that we thought he was just like the dog in the Marmaduke comics, a Great Dane in constant trouble. One day we tied the ever-barking Duke to the tree in our front yard while we ran an errand. While we were gone, a neighbor was so disgusted with Duke's constant barking that he filled a hot dog bun with Tabasco hot sauce and threw it to Duke, who naturally gulped it down quickly.

Our third child, James on his three-wheeler with a 26 HP motorcycle engine that we built from scratch. Photo from the 1970s.

My parents Ralph and Tessie Welch with our kids.

Our neighbors quickly realized how wrong they were to do that. They were terrified Duke was going to die. His tongue hung out about a foot as he gasped for air. His eyes rolled back, and he lay motionless on the grass. About a half hour later, he, thankfully, was back up on his paws.

Duke loved to run whenever James opened his pen to play and exercise the pup. One day he escaped from James and was gone for about an hour. This continued practically every day until we received a phone call from a very irate person.

"I finally found out where you guys live. You have that menacing dog," she loudly told me. "That blanked-ly-blank dog has pooped on my front step daily for two weeks. Every time I go out my front door, I step in that blankedly-blank stuff."

Shortly after that, we took Duke to "doggie heaven."

Duke is shown with Jann and James.

My Sister Cynthia

My sister Cynthia was a great believer who spoke about her faith at churches all over the country. A teacher by training, she brought hundreds of people to Christ before her death in 1975 from adenocarcinoma, a cancer that develops in cells lining glandular organs, such as the lungs, breasts, colon, prostate, stomach, pancreas, and cervix.

In Cynthia's case, she had long suffered with colitis, an inflammatory bowel disease, which turned into the cancer. In those days less was known about colitis and diet, and there were fewer treatments in general for cancer. Cynthia and Jann flew to Texas to see a doctor who treated this type of cancer nutritionally, but it was too late to really help my sister.

But it was not too late for Cynthia to help and inspire others. As she became sicker, she became stronger for the Lord. Cynthia was not one to complain because she had faith in the Lord. It was hard going to see her because she was not getting better. We felt sad knowing we were going to lose her, but we always left her bedside with our spirits raised.

The very last person Cynthia brought to Christ was one of her nurses, who noted that her dying patient was able to smile despite her suffering as she lay dying in the hospital. "I wish I had what she has," the nurse said. "She is riddled with pain but is still smiling and at peace." Instantly, that nurse became a believer and accepted Christ!

We were so sad when Cynthia passed away, and yet we were relieved because her pain was over. We knew her body was gone, but her spirit lives on because she believed in the Lord.

The Lord showed how much he loved her on the day of Cynthia's funeral. It began as a rainy day that symbolized our sadness for her loss. As the funeral procession traveled from Bethany Church in La Crosse, Wisconsin to the cemetery in La Crescent, the sun broke out and the sky turned a beautiful blue. We realized the Lord was again shining on Cynthia and blessing us.

Cynthia and her husband, Earl Good, had two sons, Kevin and Jon.

Cynthia and I were young adults in this photo in
front of our family home in La Crescent.

Left Jann, and Cynthia are shown with Kendra at a Christmas celebration in 1962. Cynthia was already sick with cancer at the time.

Chapter 8

Component Building Systems (CBS)

As our lumber business grew, we designed, estimated, built, and supplied roof rafters, laminated beams, pole barns, and roof trusses as well as houses. We started building wall components for houses on a jig table that I designed and built at the lumberyard. That jig allowed us to build components with great efficiency and quality.

Without really thinking about it, our business evolved into component home building, which turned out to be a very good opportunity for us. A component house is comprised of floor deck sections, outside wall sections that have sheathing, siding, windows, exterior doors, interior partitions, and separate roof trusses. We delivered components to the field in our semi-trucks and set them with a rented truck crane.

Our timing could not have been better. La Crescent entered a building boom so large in the 1960s and 1970s that contractors came from all over the Midwest and beyond to build houses in La Crescent. Many sought us out when they learned our prices were fair and we were dedicated to service and quality.

As dramatically as our company was growing in sales, we were careful about adding staff, doing so only when an employee was working sixty to eighty hours a week. I did not ask my workers to do anything that I would not do. I put in these same long hours working alongside them. It was only fair.

Each worker became part of our family, and we worked hard to make sure their skills matched a job with which they would be happy at work. All foremen were experienced carpenters. We encouraged workers and foremen to improve and build the business. I didn't know it at the time, but the Lord had his hand on the start of our new business.

One day when we loaded wall components on our flatbed truck, the three other men carrying the 16-by-8-ft. wall dropped their end. The result was a back injury for me that required my being rushed to the hospital for treatment.

That prompted our buying a used forklift that moved lumber materials by machine rather than by hand. It was more efficient and saved my aching back, not to mention potential injury to our employees.

Our component business grew so rapidly that we ran out of space at the lumberyard, which led to our creating CBS (**C**omponent **B**uilding **S**ystems) Homes out of Consolidated Builders Supply. We were learning, growing, and busting at the seams about the time that the La Crescent Lumber and Coal Company site became available to buy.

It was a much larger space and a perfect fit for us as our base of operations. We designed and built a huge pole barn building with a sixteen-foot-high ceiling on that site to house our new component plant.

We called our milling division Crescent Building Products. My blue Toyota truck is pictured with straight bumpers.

One employee was assigned the job of building the machinery and forty-foot-long steel jig table that I designed. Outside wall sections were built on this steel jig table, which was the same length as our semi-trailers. A steel arm on our forklift lifted the components and placed them on the trailers.

Eventually, a monorail system took the place of the forklift, making loading faster and more efficient. The monorail track system was bolted to the ceiling, traveling over each workstation to the semi loading bay. The monorail had an air hoist lift that picked up panels from the jig table, taking them to our windows, exterior doors, and siding stations, and then delivering the finished component to the semitrailer.

We expanded the new pole barn further south to house our gable end station. Here we took the gable truss and applied sheathing, siding, and rake sections. This same building housed our new truss fabrication center.

The truss area housed our truss saw-cutting equipment as well as the new truss assembly jig table. This jig table had a twenty-five-ton hydraulic C-Clamp Press System, which pressed steel plates into the wood joints of each roof truss.

All of these jigs and other specially designed equipment meant we could build houses more quickly and with uniform quality.

Building walls in the CBS plant. Workers assembling walls on the jig table that held studs in place before sheathing was applied.

This photo shows our monorail system on the left side and walls loaded into the semitrailer.

The photo shows a 40-foot, air-operated jig table that stapled sheathing to the outside wall. Our Research and Development Department developed our machines.

Losing Dad

I was playing golf one Sunday in 1970 with my friend Dick Kathan (who I served with in the Airborne) when a golf course ranger rushed out to the fairway we were on. "Go quickly, Jack," he said. "Your dad is critically ill in the hospital."

My wife Jann and I rushed to Lutheran Hospital in La Crosse, now Gundersen Health System, where we found that Dad had suffered a brain aneurysm—a ballooning of a blood vessel. He needed immediate surgery to save his life, and even with it, they could not guarantee he would make it. Sadly, the operation was not successful.

His last words as I stood holding his hand to comfort him were, "Oh, Jack."

I was devastated by the loss of my dad when he was at the very young age of sixty-five. He had been my business partner my entire career, except for those few months when I worked for Trane—and he was not just my dad; he was my very close friend.

After a huge funeral for Dad attended by many people from throughout the area, it took me three days before I regained enough composure to go back to work. When I did go back, he was in my heart and mind as we continued to build on the company that had been his dream two decades earlier.

Continued growth

As component sales grew, we purchased land from La Crescent Ready-Mix Concrete for a new deck plant and a shop for research and development. We also designed and built an overhead crane in our deck plant. The complete floor deck for each house was built in removable eight-foot-wide sections. These sections were lifted by our first overhead crane and loaded onto a flatbed semitrailer.

Our next expansion was on the former Iverson Lumber Company property. It became home to our millwork division, Crescent Building Products. This company manufactured 120 pre-hung doors daily and supplied all of the millwork products, including pre-hung exterior doors of many varieties and sizes.

The orders for housing continued to grow, which meant we needed further expansion for truss production. We purchased a multi-spindle, truss-cutting saw. This huge machine had one button that operated four saw-cutting motors, automatically changing the angles with the truss web-cutting requirements. This saw increased our truss production by 400 percent.

To facilitate lumber usage into this machine, we designed a second overhead bridge crane which supported an electric forklift. The operator handling a cable wand from the bridge crane picked up a bundled unit of lumber with the forklift and carried it over piled lumber to the multi-spindle saw-cutting machine. This saw-cutting operation in our plant was unique in the component industry.

Our final expansion was our new 80-foot-wide by 270-foot-long component plant facility. We loaded three semis at a time in that huge building, allowing us to build three to seven homes a day.

We built our third bridge crane, which included an air-operated hoist to move wall components to different stations throughout the new plant. I designed our component equipment, which our research and development department built. This allowed us to increase our efficiency, but we also ran other programs that helped us further by analyzing how many linear feet per hour was produced on a line.

Our plant also housed the most advanced heating system in the country during the late 1970s. I designed this system to grind our scrap lumber into wood chips that were blown into a silo holding tank. The bottom of the silo housed an auger, which rotated the chips into our wood-fired furnace boiler. The heated boiler water circulated into our ceiling space heaters throughout the plant. It reduced our heating bill to zero! It was a revolutionary, "green" idea for the 1970s.

The facilities also reduced fixed-overhead costs, reducing lighting expenses by 90 percent with sodium vapor lighting, which usually was used for street and highway lighting only.

In November 1979, Automation in Housing, a national trade journal for housing construction, ran a front-page story about CBS Homes. The article described our company as the most advanced component manufacturer in the country.

We Made Home Deliveries

We normally set a 1,500-square foot house with all of the components and roof trusses on an existing foundation in three and a half hours. When we left, exterior walls were finished, and the roof trusses were set. The builder's crew then took over, nailing the components together at the site and finished the roofing. They added plumbing, electrical, heating, insulation, and dry wall. After dry wall was completed, CBS Homes delivered the interior millwork package, including interior doors, trim, closet material, kitchen cabinets, vanities, and tops to the builder for installation. The builder provided carpeting and flooring to complete the home.

The first truck we used was a long, wheeled-based flatbed truck that pulled a trailer made from a used mobile home minus the house. We built a flatbed floor on top of the mobile home frame that allowed us to carry those large components to the sites. As our business grew, we purchased our first semi-tractor and two trailers. In the late 1970s before our devastating fire at CBS Homes, thirty semitrailers and six diesel tractors delivered components through a five-state area of Minnesota, Wisconsin, Iowa, Michigan, and Illinois.

The key elements that made our product successful were:

- Guaranteed prices.
- Designs engineered to prevent waste in the field and very little in the plant.

- Rapid turnaround. Salesmen estimated a house overnight and presented it the next day to the customer.
- Weather did not have an impact on the product, which meant higher quality.
- CBS Homes' components "fit together like a glove." There were no computers then it was figured out by hand.
- Efficient installation.

The first delivery of a component house went to a site seventy-five miles away from our La Crescent plant. We hired a builder for the site, which was near a river. The rectangular home was set, complete with its roof. When the owner came at noon to see our progress, he was upset. "My home is backwards. I want the front door facing the river instead of facing the street!"

I was called and came as quickly as possible. "When you come back, your home will be the way you want it," I reassured the owner.

He looked a bit unsure that we could do that, but we hired a huge crane, which picked up the whole house with straps, turned the house 180 degrees, and then replaced it on the foundation. When the owner saw what was done, he was stunned. "How did you get this house turned the way I wanted in such a short time? It's a miracle!"

Sharing our story

To build our business, we made frequent presentations at contractor meetings, where we told our story to many builders. We also had six salesmen who visited real estate agents and contractors, inviting them to look at our system that saved them time, money, and material waste. Also, we told the contractors, weather was not a factor because the home was built in our CBS building all weather plants.

We engineered and built our own trusses and wall components without the advantages of computers or even calculators. We manually calculated the load bearing for roof trusses and floor systems, I had to engineer, even though I had no formal training. Instead, I used my God given gifts to calculate moments of tension and compression and shear strength of products.

Contractors told us they appreciated the CBS Homes because the quality was higher than what they could build themselves in the field. Our houses had to be substantial enough to travel over the road—sometimes over rough roads.

The interstate system constructed in the 1950s and 1960s helped build our business by making it possible for our semis to travel within a 250-mile radius of La Crescent, Minnesota. We could get our components where they needed to go.

One marketing tool we used at CBS homes was an ad in the local paper telling readers a CBS home was going up in their area. Throngs of people came to watch. They loved to see a crane bringing in the panels and the crew assembling them together.

After ten years in the business, we hit the $1 million mark in annual sales, which would be like $2.8 million in 2012, the most recent year for which comparisons are available. At the end of 1979, our annual sales were $14 million (about $44 million in 2013 dollars).

By the end of the 1970s, we experimented with building complete bath modules with electric wiring, plumbing fixtures and piping, fan and vent; finished dry wall, finished flooring; wall, mirror and vanity, and cabinets. We included the toilet, bowl, tub, and shower; even a shower curtain.

Trappings of success

We invested in a houseboat in1976 that turned out to be the Welch family's personal Titanic. I hired a man known as Wing-dam Sam for this two-story, forty-seven-footer for us with an outside stairway and an operational fly bridge.

He built it at a very good price, which he made even better when I told him I would sell him GE appliances at cost, since we had access to them through CBS Homes.

The furniture for the boat, including rattan for the outside and the davenport, tables, and beds on the inside, came from a northern Minnesota manufacturing company.

I asked Wing-dam to train me on the boat's operation when he delivered it, but he blew off my request.

"Jack, don't worry about it," he told me. "It runs just like a car. You don't have to worry about steering it. It will steer by itself. Just turn the wheel a little bit."

I asked about bilge pumps, which would remove water in the lowest level of the boat. Wing-dam said they weren't needed, which should have raised a red flag. He also told me this boat would never sink. They said the same thing about that other ship that went down on April 15, 1912.

The Welch family boat on its maiden titanic voyage in 1976.

On our maiden voyage, we happily headed north with our three kids, my mom, Jann's mother and father, and our son's best friend. I successfully navigated the first lock and dam on the Mississippi River and then radioed the lockmaster as we approached at Alma, Wisconsin.

"Come through, Captain, the locks are open," the lockmaster said.

I had a little sketch on my console telling me how to operate the throttles and shift levels on the two engines, but I learned too late that the drawing were backwards. As I came in, the bow hit the side of the concrete wall where water is raised and lowered in the lock. Our boat then turned and swung 180 degrees heading backwards, sending little fishing boats around me scurrying away in panic before our twenty-ton boat hit them. We finally crashed into the wall, which caused our dishes to fall out of the cabinets.

The lockmaster was not happy. I must confess that after we crashed, I told Jann to go to the top deck to talk to the lockmaster. I felt like crawling under the carpet. I wanted to stay out of this. You cannot imagine the swear words that came out of his mouth. He finally told me to exit my boat backwards heading north out of the locks. We did and then headed north.

We took the crystal-clear St. Croix River where it connected with the Mississippi to go further north to Afton,

Minnesota, where a big peninsula juts out of the river. Looking down into the water, you could see all the way to the bottom, far different from the churning, murky Mississippi.

With permission to port in Afton on the peninsula, I pulled into a spot next to a beautiful, eighty-foot-long houseboat called the Funny Farm II. I struck up a conversation with the owner, a banker.

As I was chatting with the banker, Jann was doing dishes after breakfast. She opened the boat's hatch and hand-pumped the toilet waste into what we thought was a holding tank.

To the horror of the banker and me, we saw everything coming out of our toilet into that pristine St. Croix River. The banker immediately was angry, threatening to report us. I cupped my hands, yelling *"Stop Jann!"* but she was so busy pumping that she did not hear me.

Finally, this guy backed his boat out, leaving in a fury. We had no idea there was no holding tank in our boat.

After a busy day, we all retired and slept well. The next morning, my mom was puzzled by what she saw. "Afton moved," she said.

"Afton moved?"

At night we saw it on the right side, but in the morning Afton was on the left. Horror of horrors, one anchor had gotten loose, which caused us to swing about 180 degrees again!

With our vacation nearing its end, we headed south into Lake Pepin where we ported overnight at Lake City. The next morning I called the weather station to check on conditions south of us and was told it was clear sailing. As we sailed on Lake Pepin, my daughter and I were on the top deck where I operated the boat. All of a sudden, eighteen-foot waves washed over the top of our boat.

Jann called me to come down quickly to the cabin area, which was filling up with water. Everyone grabbed cans and buckets to get the water out, but it was gaining on us. We couldn't bucket fast enough. There were no bilge pumps installed to pump out the water.

I called the Coast Guard for help and was told we were on the backside of a sudden tornado that came up unexpectedly. The Coast Guard couldn't assist us— there were too many boats going down. We could see the mouth of the Mississippi River and that it was calm just beyond it, but we couldn't get there.

The waves came over so fast that the anchor rope caught in the propeller of the engine. We couldn't cut it free. At that point I realized we were losing the battle and were taking on too much water. I headed to shore. We followed the rocky coastline until the boat became so heavy with storm water that I decided we must abandon ship by Camp La Coupoles on Lake Pepin.

I told everyone to put on life jackets. Jann had the presence of mind to tell everyone to get their shoes on, and she took the essentials like wallets and purses, throwing them into plastic bags to carry with us. All nine of us spread out so that anything that could be saved was handed off to each other in a brigade to get it to shore. Even the non-swimmers walked bravely over the huge slippery rocks to shore.

The boat went down near Camp La Coupoles on Lake Pepin. The aerial was the only remaining sign above the water. Our nephew Kevin, who was seventy miles away, said he broke a land speed record coming from La Crescent to get us in a large enclosed truck.

The next day, I called a marine operator in Wabasha, Minnesota, to see about raising our boat. As he pumped the water out, the boat raised itself. There were no holes in the hull, but we still needed to redo the entire boat and engines, costing $50,000.00. We made sure a holding tank and bilge pumps were added in the boat remodel.

We called our boat The New Life, with the goal of it being a conversation starter about our personal relationships with Christ. We had to sell it in 1981 after the CBS fire.

Wright Homes

To the success of CBS homes during the late 1970s, we added a new division called Wright Homes, which delivered everything needed for a specific house to the work site. We supplied all the materials for the sill plates, floor joists and sheathing. All the precut studs, assembled corners, window and interior door bucks and framing lumber. We manufactured the roof trusses and supplied all the roofing, soffit materials, outside wall and roof sheathing, siding, and windows. We also provided the heating, electric, and plumbing packages. The home owner who had mechanical skills could then build his home on the site. The second truck delivered the insulation and drywall package. The final truck was the millwork package which included all the interior prehung doors, casing, base, cabinets, counter tops.

Our motto was, "We do what's Wright! You do what's left!" It referred to savings of about 29 percent on the cost of a precut home by putting in "sweat equity," as Robert M. Mason, part owner and division manager, described it.

By completing some work themselves, homeowners reduced the down payment financial institutions required for a loan. Since everything was precut for just what was needed, there was much less waste. With these savings, customers built the home of their dreams, instead of scaling down their house.

Each division—CBS Homes and Wright Homes—had seven or eight sales people, and together our company peaked at 120 employees. We expanded our facilities all over La Crescent with 3 1/2 acres of buildings under roof. We were so successful that we were rewarded with a trip to Hong Kong and Japan for selling the most General Electric appliances in the area. Another time we were honored for sales of Jenn-Air appliances in Minnesota.

CBS Homes became well known in several states. The Minnesota Chamber of Commerce had a contest for all Minnesota businesses to identify our state's top companies. We were invited to an event in the Radisson Ballroom in Minneapolis, Minnesota, where we presented a slideshow about our business.

Out of thousands in the state, CBS Homes was named the second-best business in Minnesota in 1976—a great honor! Rose Totino's Pizza, which dated back to 1951 and was created by the daughter of Italian immigrants, won first place.

When our business became highly successful, I felt I could do no wrong. We were at the top of our game—or so I thought. As the saying goes, "Pride comes before the fall."

As you will read, love of my wife and children did not keep me from doing things that were nothing short of shameful in my private life. ***"Wine, women and song" was my motto—and I could not sing!***

Chapter 9

Becoming a Believer

Like most families in the United States, we considered ourselves to be Christians because we went to church each Sunday? In my case we went to the Presbyterian Church in La Crescent, which was one of a hundred that Sheldon Jackson, a nineteenth-century Presbyterian missionary established in western United States during his million miles of travels. Ours was the first church bell he rang west of the Mississippi River.

As a young lad I remember our church being raised up in order to put a basement under it. This small, antique church could only hold eighty to one hundred people, which made it hard to recruit and retain ministers.

What I heard in church did not stick with me when I left the building, especially as an adult. I lived a very different life because I wasn't a genuine believer—I had not accepted Christ as my savior.

My mom was a believer. She had accepted Christ; my dad had not. But one time they went together to a Billy Graham Crusade in Minneapolis, where Dad suddenly went to the front and accepted Jesus. I didn't know about it at the time. Like politics, you just didn't talk about religion much in those days.

I cut a pretty wide swath when I was younger. As we were growing the business, I worked very long hours, but not as long as Jann thought. Working was my cover for my bad behavior.

As I said in the previous chapter, I was into **wine, women and song and I couldn't sing.** I went to bed many nights ashamed of myself, yet I could not stop. I had no regulator on me, even though I went to church every Sunday (but I did not know Christ).

I was getting deeper and deeper and deeper into a twenty-foot hole with a ten-foot ladder. I had no idea my life was falling apart. If I continued on that wrong path, I know our marriage would have ended in divorce. It's not what I wanted, but I think Jann would have left me.

I still loved my wife and kids, but I was a shameful hypocrite. I thought there was something wrong with me but had no idea what to change or how to do it. I was ruled by my own selfish desires. Each night I spent at the office, the lust for the flesh was conquering my heart. I was weaving a web of self-destruction. I was driven by satanic desires not knowing that the Lord would take away all that I had built up. My heart became callous through my addiction. I was trying to find something? I had an empty feeling or a void in my heart!

Around 1970, we had friends who invited us to a weekly couple's Bible study in La Crescent. Several times when I was supposed to go with Jann to those meetings, I jumped into my truck and went instead to a tavern.

My best friend Bruce (Nels) Nelson, who had been the best man in our wedding, invited me to go to church on Sunday evenings in La Crosse, Wisconsin. I told him I had no interest in his church, which I thought would be enough for him to leave me alone. I fought it tooth and nail. Bruce would not give up.

Sometime later, he called me and asked if we could go as couples to a movie on Sunday night. He picked us up, but then passed the downtown La Crosse theaters. He mentioned a North Side theater called the Bijou, but also drove by it. We stopped in front of the Bethany Church located in a former railroad depot in La Crosse.

"Well, Jack," he said. "I got you here on a Sunday night. Let's go inside."

He had set that trap with Jann's help. She knew it was the only way to actually get me there. Flustered and upset, I agreed on one condition—that we sit in the back and I could get out quickly if things went south. I expected to make a fast exit but did not.

I saw people singing like they meant every word. They sang with a sincere, convicted heart. When Pastor David Martin gave his sermon, I thought this was a different kind of church. He spoke the truths of the Scripture like I hadn't heard before. Afterwards, a man practically jumped over five pews to shake hands with us to welcome us to the church.

Bruce Nelson was my best man at my wedding, while Marti, the woman who later became his wife, was an attendant.

"What did you think Jack?" Nels asked me after the service. I told him that it felt like everyone sincerely believed what he or she sang and heard. He agreed, adding, "I became a believer through this church."

From that day on we went Sunday mornings to our church in La Crescent and then on Sunday evenings to

Bethany. My first impressions remained—Bethany was a place where prayer was heartfelt.

Our two families were part of a larger group of friends who got together regularly for corn feeds and pizza parties. When our two families got together several times a week, Bruce and I would argue for the sport of it, each time taking different political positions.

Then Bruce developed cancer, one that he could not beat. Within a few months, this 190-pound man was down to about 100 pounds. One day when I visited him, he asked me to pray for him. "Bruce, I've never prayed out loud a day in my life. I wouldn't know what to say."

"Say something," he responded and I prayed with him in his bedroom.

Now the scene changed, later in the hospital in La Crosse about two hours before Bruce passed away in 1972, his minister came up to me and said, "Jack, I don't know what you prayed about at Bruce's house but it really affected him. It really got to him; it changed his whole demeanor."

At that moment a warm feeling came over my sin-sickened heart, tears freely flowed down my checks, and I felt a complete change in me. At that moment I gave my life to Christ and accepted the Lord as my savior. Jann believes Bruce felt comfort and was at peace because I finally softened my heart and prayed with my best friend.

Accepting Christ through his grace made such an impact on me that my old evil thoughts and desires completely left me. In my old restless life, nothing satisfied me. My futile search ended when I found Christ. When I asked the Lord for forgiveness, a great peace enveloped my whole being.

The national Presbyterian Synod closed our local church, which was torn down. Shortly thereafter, we joined another main-line church in town. As my heart changed and I became more excited for the Lord, I wanted to teach adult Sunday school. Each Sunday as I opened, I shared with my class on *how to receive Christ and become a believer in him.*

One Sunday, the minister's wife sat in the class listening. She suddenly stood up and stormed out of the room, slamming the door behind her. I excused myself to the class, saying I had to find out what was wrong. I caught up with her and asked, "Did I say something to offend you?"

"You certainly did," she said. "You can't tell people to accept Christ in this church!!"

It was at that point I realized that we were attending the wrong church. You can't encourage acceptance of Christ in a Christian church? It just seemed so un-Christian-like to me. Our family left the church, and we started attending Bethany full time.

Bethany has a long history, beginning on the North Side of La Crosse in 1932 as the Bethany Gospel Tabernacle, a name that changed to Bethany Evangelical Free Church in 1951. Pastor David Martin, who came to Bethany in 1970, used music so effectively as part of the service that this aspiring little church began gaining members.

Soon, we had a standing-room-only "crisis." That led to the construction of a new church on County Highway B, which has been Bethany's home since September 1, 1974.

It was at Bethany that I learned true wealth is not measured by your personal wealth and possessions but by who you are in Christ. In John 14:6, Jesus says, **"I am the Way, the Truth and the Life. No one comes to the Father except through Me."** First John 5:13, He says, **"I write these things to you who believe in the name of the Son of God so that you may know that you have eternal life."**

I experienced a true reversal in my life; my wants were now satisfied, it was no longer about me but about him. One day while attending a church board meeting, each member gave their testimony. When my turn came, I said, "I had accepted Christ into my life totally, my sin sickened heart was now satisfied, my bad past is now forgiven.

One of the board members after I completed my testimony said, when you're out and about and you don't see me, "Jack, but I watch every move you make. What he said was, one should walk the walk and talk the talk. Never do something that would cause someone to stumble.

My restless life of searching for something I could not find ended when I fully accepted Christ. The following Bible verse from Galatians 2:20 has become very real to me: *"I have been crucified with Christ and I no longer live, but Christ lives in me. The life I lived by flesh, I now live by faith through Christ who loves me and died for me."*

Chapter 10

A Change of Heart and Spirit in My Business

My life changed when my best friend died of cancer in 1972. Until that time, I thought everything centered on me. When his pastor described the impact of my praying with Nels, it went straight to my heart. A warm feeling came over my total being, and I felt a joy and peace that passes all understanding.

The opening of my eyes and heart to the truth about what I found through Christ reminds me of the Bible passage about the scales falling off of Paul's blinded eyes.

Paul was on the road to Damascus to kill more Christians when the risen Christ threw him off his horse onto the ground. He heard the voice of Jesus saying, "Why do you persecute me?" Paul became blinded for three days. The risen

Jesus commanded Ananias to go to Paul (Saul) and remove the scales off his blinded eyes and restore his sight. Then Ananias went to the house and entered it. Placing his hands on Saul, he said: "Brother Saul, the Lord—Jesus, who appeared to you on the road as you were coming here—has sent me so that you may see again and be filled with the Holy Spirit." Immediately, something like scales fell from Saul's eyes, and he could see again. He got up and was baptized, and after taking some food, he regained his strength. Acts 9:1–20 (NIV)

As a believer, I made a new beginning with my family, friends and business. Instead of **"I"** or **"me"** in the center, **I took a servant's position with Christ at the center of my life.** In Psalms 62:6 tells me: **"He alone is my rock and my salvation; he is my fortress, I will not be shaken."**

Philippians 4:13 tells me: **"I can do all things through Christ, who strengthens me."**

I had no idea the impact this change in me would have on my business until one day in 1978 when I was working at my desk at CBS Homes. I looked up and saw a man standing there. He seemed an ordinary man about age thirty, wearing casual clothes.

"Can I help you?" I asked.

"Have you taken anyone on lately?" he asked.

Not sure what he meant, I said, "Yes, we've hired some people in our plant."

"No. You are way off."

"We've hired some people in the office." "That's not what I'm talking about." "I've taken on Christ."

"That is it. If you keep Christ in your heart and be obedient to him, your business will get to be the largest component home manufacturer in the nation!"

Then he left without leaving his name. I ran after him, but he was gone. I asked my secretary by the front door if she had seen him, and she had not. I went out the back door and asked different guys working in the plant, but they had not seen him. No one had.

My only explanation was that he had been an angel unaware—my angel—there to remind me that Christ was more important in my life than my business.

The business did grow so much that articles were written about our company, locally and across the country. The *La Crosse Tribune* did a story when we began our pre-cut home packages under the Wright Homes division name with the slogan, "We do what's Wright. You do what's left." That meant the homeowner became the contractor.

In November 1979, *Manufactured Housing*, a trade journal for the industry, did a two-page spread on us because our new facilities more than doubled our production capabilities. The facilities also reduced fixed overhead costs, cutting down lighting costs by 90 percent using sodium vapor lighting. Also, the new plant had a heating systems that saved about 80 percent in heating costs.

We designed and built a green energy heating system that heated our new plant. We chipped all of our waste lumber pieces and blew them into our steel silo. We installed an auger feed that fed the furnace through a thermostat control to heat our plant. That kind of green heating system was unheard-of in 1979. We were the most advanced housing company in the country.

We projected continued growth because of the new plant our sales "by 2014 standards would equal $42 million."

Writing in *Automation in Housing & Systems Building News*, Richard W. Douglass noted CBS had grown from building one house a week to five a day in fifteen years. "This is why John (Jack) Welch, CBS founder and president, is optimistic about this year and the years ahead. CBS has prepared itself to shelter market whichever turn the economy takes."

Sadly and ironically, this article came out in March 1980, about two months after the fire. We had been interviewed in the fall of 1979, when I was overjoyed then by our progress in business.

Automation in Housing
& SYSTEMS BUILDING NEWS

The Management Magazine for Manufactured Housing and Volume Builders   March 1980

INNOVATIVELY DESIGNED mobile homes and double section modulars await shipment at the Schult Homes plant and headquarters in Middlebury, IN.

At Schult Homes:
Innovation In Housing Units Is Main Target

By Jan Noble, Sr.

"THE SECRET OF SUCCESS is constancy to purpose," said Disraeli in 1872.

It's not coincidence that constancy to purpose is a principle that can be felt strongly when talking to Walter E. Wells, president of Schult Homes headquartered in Middlebury, IN.

"The company was founded on the premise that the 'customer is all mighty,' " says Wells. "And, we continue this philosophy today."

Schult Homes is the oldest mobile home manufacturer in the country. It all began when Wilbur Schult went to Chicago in 1933 and bought a Covered Wagon trailer to set up a dealership in Elkhart, IN. After one year of selling Covered Wagon trailers, Schult formed a partnership with Walter Wells, father of the current president, Walter E. Wells. The two began manufacturing their own trailers.

From that beginning, two major

Continued on Page 16

ALSO IN THIS ISSUE:

At Affordable Luxury Homes, Inc.:
Fuel Conscious Buyers Respond to Foam Insulated Sandwich Panels

By Don Carlson

THE QUICK TRANSITION of America's energy problem from an 'annoyance' to a 'critical crunch' is swiftly increasing the home sales potential for Affordable Luxury Homes, Inc., Markle (near Fort Wayne), Indiana.

Why? Because the company builds an architecturally attractive closed panel line of homes which utilize high-efficiency expanded polystyrene (EPS) insulation blocks as the core of its laminated sandwich panel walls. Depending on the buyer's choice, the walls can be 4", 6", or 8" thick with 3½", 5½", or 7½" slabs of polystyrene inside — rated for high density at R-4.35 per inch at 75° F* — to help slash owners heating and air conditioning costs to 'no problem' levels. Depending on the final finish, the exterior

THICKNESS OF EPS FOAM in sandwich panel walls of 4", 6" and 8" dimensions is shown by Karol Cossairt, president, Affordable Luxury Homes, Inc.

walls can have up to seven layers of building materials with R-ratings almost as high as R-45 for the

Continued on Page 8

CBS Expands Profit Centers With Multi-Pronged Program

By Richard W. Douglass

GROWING FROM A PRODUCTION output of one house a week to 10 houses a day over a 15-year span is the capsuled history of CBS (Component Building Systems) in La Crescent, MN, across the Mississippi River from La Crosse, WI.

As you may surmise, CBS is no biggie in dollars and unit output, but it knows no perimeters in imagination and ingenuity and ability to adapt its product to the market.

That is why John (Jack) Welch, CBS founder and president, is optimistic about this year and the years ahead. CBS has prepared itself to ex-

Continued on Page 12

CBS MANAGEMENT TEAM: (left to right) Richard (Dick) Stokely, sales manager, Les Snuggerod, director of engineering, John (Jack) Welch, president, Gerald Roob, operations, and Don Schumacher, general manager/production.

A national publication magazine: CBS Homes front page feature.

A Special Section On
MANUFACTURED HOUSING

New Facility Doubles Panel Production

Just six months after opening a new 23,500-square-foot panel-making plant, CBS Homes is coping, happily, with full-tilt production. Specializing in building component systems, the La Crescent, Minn.-based firm has realized a production rate that is more than 2½ times greater than its former facility's output.

CBS president John W. Welch said, "In our previous panel-making line, we were able to produce panels at a maximum rate of 6½ linear feet per man-hour of labor. With the new plant, our production rate has gone up to 16 linear feet per man-hour."

The panel-making facility, measuring about 80x290 feet, represents an investment of about $1.2 million. It will likely mean an increase in the average number of employees from about 70 to nearly 150. Using a fleet of 30 open-top trailers, the shipping radius for the new plant will be extended to 200 miles and as much as 300 for special larger projects.

Dan Baldridge, special projects coordinator for CBS, anticipates an increase in the new plant's capability from about two houses a day to about 10 houses a day. Expectations are that last year's roster of 85 to 90 builder/dealers

in four states would be increasing this year to about 135 or 140.

The new panel-making line at CBS is laid out so that fabrication work starts out on conveyor tables down one side of the building. Then, with the help of overhead hoists, the line makes a U-turn and comes back along the other side with panels sections held in near-vertical mobile racks for window and siding installation. The air-operated, skate-wheel conveyor tables, the mobile holding racks and the tilt-down siding application racks were all designed by CBS and fabricated in the company's own metal-working shop.

System specifics

In highlighting how the panel-making equipment works, Welch noted, "We start out with the conveyor system tables where we frame our walls and apply sheathing. This system involves a fully air-operated jig that will handle panels up to about 42 feet long. Input to the jig includes subcomponents made in a separate subcomponents shop and brought in on pallets with forklifts. Input also includes window-and-door buck sub-assemblies made right here.

"These units are skated down the conveyor tables to drop into their proper

positions in the panel being made. Then, studs and plates are filled in and a pushbutton operates a lock-in press to hold the complete framing section aligned and square in what we call 'gun-barrel straightness' for nailing. Then, our bridge-type sheathing nailer comes along and is air-operated for both movement and stapling. It can handle nailing of panels from 2x4s with just half-inch sheathing up to 2x6s with full 1-inch thick sheathing."

The sheathed panels at the U-turn in the fabricating line are picked up by an electric hoist and shifted into the mobile holding racks which are moved manually to the window-door installation area. They are then moved to a holding area for transfer to the siding application racks by the overhead crane. These four racks, like the holding racks, are fabricated of steel, but the siding racks fold down to a horizontal position. This permits horizontal sidings to be applied in the near-vertical position, but allows vertical sidings in the flat horizontal position.

"The objective of the mobile holding racks and the siding application racks is to accommodate the slower rate of siding application," Welch said. "This is

Following U-turn where panel sections are hoisted into mobile racks that hold the panels in near-vertical position, the racks move in floor channels to the window-door installation area. Beyond is the rack holding area and, at the far end, the siding-application area.

178/MANUFACTURED HOUSING NOVEMBER, 1978

Featured Story on our new plant, 80 ft. x 290 ft. 23,200 square feet plus offices and storage area.

A Difficult Time

A contractor in Dakota County near Minneapolis had been a good customer of ours for a number of years, paying promptly for one house package a month. He increased his order to two houses a month, but by the end of the second month, he owed us for all four houses. Instead of paying us the $250,000 due us, he wrote me a letter saying he had filed for bankruptcy.

At that point I told my salesman to bring back the warranty deed for the houses so we could finish and sell the houses to recover our losses. The contractor sued us for the profits of the houses for which he had not paid.

When we went to trial in Dakota County Courthouse in Hastings, Minnesota, he had two lawyers and six expert witnesses. I arrived with my manager and head accountant. I did not have an attorney so I cross-examined his attorneys and the witnesses. The trial lasted for two days, and the judge awarded us the case.

The contractor became so mad that he came up to me afterwards and said, "Jack, I am going to destroy you. You wait and see. You will regret winning this case."

I put aside thoughts about what he had said, although it was certainly chilling at the time.

And Then It Happened

On that early morning of January 17, 1980, my world changed as I knew it. I was preparing for a talk with our Wright Homes Sales staff. I wrapped up about 11:30 PM, locked the door to the office, and went directly home. About 2:00 AM my wife and I were startled from a sound sleep. The dispatcher from the La Crescent Fire Department said to my wife, "You have a fire at CBS Homes." I said, *"Oh, it's probably a wastebasket burning."* The dispatcher called back and said, *"Jack, you better get down here! Your whole place is on fire!"* When I went out the front door of our home, the sky was crimson red, and I knew I had it! I broke a land speed record getting there. I was powerless to rescue my records.

CBS Homes was reduced to six inches of ashes from a fire that gutted our three main buildings not to mention our office, equipment, and house plans. Prior to the fire we had just completed construction of the North Plant. This new, 30,000-square-foot building had the capacity of producing five houses per day. Not one house was built in the plant before the fire. All other buildings became inoperative, such as the huge deck plant, Crescent Building Products Millwork plant and warehouse, thirty semitrailers, six semi tractors, several bridge cranes, and three fork lifts. In addition, the fire destroyed all the sawing equipment at Hydro Air Truss fabricating: the automatic multi spindle truss saw, the monorail system, and the automatic multigang stapling sheathing machine.

My loss was devastating. I personally owned forty-five apartments in Minnesota and Wisconsin and 6.22 acres in downtown St Paul, Minnesota. We had plans set to build ninety-six apartments with garages on that site.

I had Five Franchise Country Kitchen Restaurants in Iowa plus an operative Country Kitchen in Ankeny, Iowa. **I personally lost $19 million because of the fire. But what I personally lost was a mere pittance compared to finding eternal life through Christ.**

As reported in local newspaper, there were more than fifty firefighters and trucks pouring water on the fire for over two days. Everything was swimming in water.

A few days after this devastating fire, my wife and I were with another couple, walking through the sea of cooled ashes that had once been our multimillion-dollar business. All that was left of La Crescent's largest employer were three-plus acres of ashes. Then we came to an area that had a rise in the ashes eighteen inches by three feet square. I bent down and picked up a piece of insulation that had fallen from the ceiling. The fire had destroyed everything except the bottom of the third drawer, which was charred around the perimeter of ***The Holy Bible***. When I picked up the Bible and flipped through the pages

I found no burn marks, water marks, or even the smell of fire. As I said earlier in this book,

IT WAS A MIRACLE! GOD HAD PROTECTED HIS WORD!

Thought: My office was twenty-four feet by twelve feet. In the room were our board table, my desk, and credenza. On the wall were **thirty-five memorabilia items that I received on serving on different committees around the area. They all melted to nothing in the fire. The only thing that really counts in life is the Word, the Bible itself!**

Suspicious Fire

There was no question the fire was intentionally set, meaning arson.

About two weeks after the fire, La Crescent Fire Chief David Schroeder held a press conference to announce the fire was intentionally set.

According to a February 2, 1980, story in the *La Crosse Tribune*, Roger Jeming, assistant state fire marshal in Minnesota, led the investigation. Also on the team were William McDonald, La Crescent fire marshal; Dick Johnson, La Crescent police chief; and Dennis Fier, an investigator with the state Bureau of Crimina1.[20] They found the fire was set in two places—inside the administration building and the other in the warehouse.

I knew I would be a suspect because the owner is always suspected in these cases. Also, the prime rate[21]—the interest rate banks charge their best customers—hit 15.25 percent in December 1979 and went to record high of 20.5 percent in December 1980. Compare that with October 2014 when it was 3.25 percent. Mortgage money reached 21 percent in 1979, which meant you couldn't give a house away in those days. But we also had created a business that could build homes much more efficiently than any builder in the area. We knew we had a future—at least before the fire.

One of the first things I did after the fire was to volunteer to take a polygraph (lie detector test), even though the results are not admissible in court. I wanted the state and local fire marshals to have confidence that I did not start the fire. All I asked was that I could have the best polygraph tester in the state of Minnesota. I didn't want a novice who might not know the right questions to ask.

I traveled to St. Paul, Minnesota (the capital of the state), and they hooked me up to the machine that recorded respiration, perspiration, heart rate, and other indicators of truthfulness. I felt like a criminal going through the test, but it had to be done and I had a real peace about the process. He said, he had to get me to lie so he would know when I was being truthful. He asked me **"Do you believe in God?" I said, "Absolutely."** When I ask the question, **"Do I believe in God"? You say "No,"** and I will note your physical response. He then proceeded to ask questions. "Did you start the fire?" I said, **"No."** "Did you have anybody start the fire?" I said **"No."** "Did you hire any relation to start the fire?" I said **"No."** During the twenty questions, the machine marked a straight line on the graph paper until he asked me, "Do you believe in God?" When I said **"No," as I was instructed to do, the polygraph line on the machine jumped right off the page. The chief polygrapher then said, "From the findings of that test, "*You did not start the fire!*"**

When I returned to La Crescent, the state and local fire marshals asked if I would give them the names of people who might have started the fire. One name given was the contractor from Minneapolis who became irate after we won the lawsuit against him. It was chilling; the contractor had threatened me, but then I forgot about it until two weeks later when CBS Homes was reduced to six inches of ashes.

In the end, I was told he was likely the guilty party. But there would be no way to bring him to trial in the case. The fire marshals said; "they had found this contractor had once owned two restaurants that had mysteriously burned in the past."

Among the articles in the *La Crosse Tribune* was one that quoted Wally Collins, assistant fire marshal for the state of Minnesota, who said arson is one of the hardest crimes to detect and prosecute. According to the Tribune article, Collins was quick to add he was not speaking about CBS Homes.

"It is a very tough crime to convict someone on," Collins said. "You have to work like crazy to get a statement from someone admitting to the crime. It often takes a huge amount of hours to come up with an airtight case."

Notes

20 Fire chief calls CBS blaze arson," *La Crosse Tribune*, February 2, 1980

21 PrimeRate:HistoricalData,http://mortgage-x.com/general/Indexes/prime.asp

Chapter 11

Rising From Ashes

When something as devastating as a fire happens, you go through stages of grief just as you do after any other loss. There's shock, anger, sorrow, depression, and ultimately you find a way to accept what has happened and go on. At first you can't comprehend the devastation.

It's hard to put into words what happened after the fire. I was fifty-two years old and had lost everything I had worked for in the last twenty-five years. I went into a horrible depression, having no idea where I would go or what I would do. Everything I had was in ashes. That was not a good place to be.

It was so difficult to tell our coworkers—people we considered to be friends and like family—that we could no longer employ them.

We cared for them, and they cared about us. We had worked hard together, pitching in to get the jobs done and yet we also had time for fun. One measure of this relationship is that I still run into former workers who are eager to get together again to talk about the good times we had at CBS Homes. Many told us it was the best place they have ever worked.

Thankfully, Jann was a registered nurse who had gone back to working full time in surgery at Lutheran Hospital in La Crosse on January 7, 1980.

We thought we were covered by our insurance. We had Builder's risk, Liability, and Business Interruption insurance. We had all our machinery covered—much that we had developed ourselves and all the buildings and equipment. It was all destroyed by fire.

The fire gutted our three main buildings and our office. We also lost several semitrailers, fork lifts, our hydro-air press, our hydro-air truss saw, all of our panel and siding jigs, many saws and the monorail system.

The fire destroyed the heart of our business! What remained were off premise from the fire and became inoperable. Remaining were the deck plant, millwork plant, and our new building called the "North Plant."

Everything in the office was destroyed, including 2,000 home plans—despite their being in what we thought was a fire-safe room. There were no computers then—all accounting records, which were on paper, were gone. It added up to millions of dollars lost.

In January 1980, we met on the forty-seventh floor of the IDS building in Minneapolis, Minnesota. Our insurance carrier brought with him about thirty lawyers and agents, who represented different segments of our total fire insurance policy.

We all sat at what seemed to be a fifty-foot-long table. They all sat on one side of the table while our group of five sat opposite them. With me to represent CBS Homes, was our head attorney and his assistant; our bookkeeper, and our manager. Our fire claim was in the multi-millions.

We were outgunned during this session that went from 7:30 a.m. to around 10:30 p.m., when we finally caved in to an agreement that did not give us anything near what our business was worth. We tried to get business interruption coverage, but the insurance company would not pay it, even though our firm employed 120 workers and was now down to ten or fifteen. We had to keep a few key people if we had even a hope of starting up again.

It was devastating. The bank called all the loans and notes due. When we got through with all the insurance settlement, we did not have the capital to start up again.

The bank held an auction on the remnants of the very fine equipment that were the keys to our success. They sold for pennies on the dollar. A forty-foot, air-operated jig table that allowed us to efficiently build outside wall components went for a mere forty dollars for use as a boat dock. It just about drove me wild to see give-away prices for items that we worked so hard to achieve. It also was an emotional trauma for my wife and our children to go through the stress of the fire.

Trying to Make a Living after the Fire

By September 1981, we announced the closing of CBS homes, NRG Homes, and Wright Homes. To make up their losses from the fire, a major bank lender proceeded to take all of my pledged assets—property that secures a debt. The lender possesses the asset, but doesn't own it unless a default occurs. The bank's new president called our notes due, along with many other businesses in the area.

I will never forget the horrible experience I had as I was driving my car through downtown La Crosse. The bank vice president saw me, stepped in front of my car, and then opened the passenger door to tell me, "I'm confiscating your Lincoln to complete your pledged assets."

I told him he could not take my car or my house under Minnesota law. I was frustrated and upset, knowing that we once had such a strong relationship with the former bank president. This was the same bank that, before the fire, eagerly lent us millions of dollars, which we had always paid back on time. But this bank was now under new leadership that did not consider old relationship

Chapter 12

Starting Metrohome Corporation

After the CBS Homes was destroyed by fire, we joined Amway, a global, direct sale marketing company that primarily sells products in health, beauty, and home care markets. Most memorable for me was an Amway seaweed product for golf courses that was supposed to keep greens green.

Rich in carbohydrates because seaweed naturally is high in sugars, it was supposed to reduce maintenance costs. It sounded good to me at a meeting I attended, so I sold it throughout the Midwest. The grass greens thrived on it, I told prospective customers. It did grow quickly—until it turned brown. My customers were very angry because it killed their courses.

Amway founder Rich De Vos, saw the impact of the product and pulled it off the market. He replaced it with a much-improved version, but I was no longer representing it.

It was another blow to me during this time—another product had gone so wrong. I could not have felt lower.

My depression was so bad that I couldn't open the door to our house; I just stayed inside feeling miserable. My wife Jann seeing my deep depression, gently suggested one day that I get out and do something, like building houses.

I could not go back to the component business because we did not have the funds for start-up. Jann suggested I stick-build houses.

That venture was called NRG Homes, which built high quality, energy-efficient homes. "We tightened up the home, putting in more insulation and gearing toward energy conservation," I was quoted as saying in a *La Crosse Tribune* article a year after the fire. "We're looking forward to the 1980s. We're going back to the basics, a smaller Volkswagen-type of home. The luxuries of the 1970s may be gone because the cost is so extremely high."

The fall of 1981 found me starting a new contracting business called Metrohome Corporation. I started it with no money—in fact it had an $80,000 debt carried over from the CBS Homes fire. The only truck I had was my blue Toyota pickup. Our dining room table was my office.

A prospective client asked us to bid on millwork for his house because of our previous millwork business. I told him that we were starting Metrohome and wondered if we could bid on the entire house. He agreed, and I won the contract for the home that my son-in-law, Jon Sopher, and I built.

Looking back, I realize how the Lord was again involved in getting our business started. Once a house is completed, you have something to use for advertising and a springboard for future construction jobs. Desperate for money I went to a La Crosse man who was then president of a Fortune 500 company and who was known for investing privately in businesses in need of capital. I desperately needed $80,000 to pay for loans remaining from CBS Homes' fire. Without money, there was no way I could start another business.

I went to see this man with a profit-and-loss statement in hand. He took one look at it and said, "This is terrible. You don't have any assets. All you have are liabilities."

"That is exactly why I am here. I know a bank will not loan me the money," I told him, adding that I was determined to rebuild my business.

He told me to redo the statement and return in two weeks. When I returned, he said it was even worse than the first statement. He then told me he had to go into a meeting..

I sat right there at his desk. I didn't move. I was praying, saying, **"Lord you have to get this loan for me. I need the money really bad."**

I looked up and saw the man, who had left his meeting and was again standing in the doorway. "Jack, I'm going to loan you the money," he said, adding, "With all of your liabilities, I found the asset."

"Where are the assets?" I asked.

"You are going to be the asset," he said. "If you miss one payment, I'll take over the business and you'll have nothing."

I repaid that loan within three years.

In business, it is essential to find people who believe in you. You also need a bank or lender who will look beyond numbers and trust you as this investor had done for me.

It Was another Miracle

We ran the business on a shoestring in those early days. My blue Toyota pickup had a broken starter, but I had no money to repair it. I went to one meeting in which I had to keep the truck running for the entire two hours for fear it would not start again.

On another occasion, I drove by a job site where a cement truck was stuck in mud. I went up to the driver and told him that if he had a chain I could help him get out with my little blue Toyota pickup. He looked doubtful, but I said I could get enough momentum on the blacktop street to pull him out.

I got everything all lined up, tightened the chain, moving my truck and his truck forward until my engine killed. His truck kept moving, crashing into my back bumper, bending it forward. The force restarted my engine, which propelled my truck forward quickly. The chain snapped tight, severely bending my back bumper backwards like a horseshoe.

My brother-in-law Lynn Witt and I took that same truck to see a prospective client in Warrens, Wisconsin. This couple in the cranberry business wanted a $1.5 million home.

As I was driving there, Lynn was following the site map. Suddenly he yelled, "Turn right here!" I turned so fast that I hit a curb, which sent my truck airborne about fifteen feet. When we came to a stop, it pushed my poor abused front bumper inward. With my front bumper going one way and the rear bumper the other way, it was no surprise that the couple chose another contractor to build their house.

After we built a number of homes, we entered the La Crosse Area Builders Parade of Homes, winning awards for the quality and creativity of our work. That helped us tremendously in marketing to prospective clients.

By the fourth year, things were going very well. We became very successful, building about twenty-five high-quality houses a year. We organized three crews—two crews framed and one crew finished. We built houses, apartments, condos, and offices. We built one site that had three office complexes. Metrohome occupied one office in the second complex.

This was the Metrohome office, now occupied by my son Brent; With Welshire Capital

A typical home design built by Metrohome

The Metrohome office consisted of our plan designer (CAD) Computer Aid Design operator Jon Knudson, our Accountant Mary Lynn, and my son-in-law Jon Sopher, who worked sales and managed the crews while I estimated all the jobs and sales.

I sold Metrohome to a former home owner.

Over the years my wife and I bought back some of the apartments that we formerly owned.

I became interested in purchasing Lancer Apartments in La Crescent, Minnesota. These ninety-six apartments located on six and a half acres of land, were built with CBS Home components in the late 1970s.We bought the complex in 2004, and we had an on-site manager managing the complex.

Most of the apartments needed renovation because of their poor condition. During the process of repairing the units, a former Trane Company engineer became interested in buying our apartments, which we sold to him in 2007.

The Lord in My Business

Each morning when I woke up, I prayed, "Lord allow me to do the business that you wish me to do in a rightful way. Allow the words to come into me. Keep me free of external bombardments so I can stay on track for you." I was not asking God for money, but for the management, organizational, and selling skills I needed each day. Keeping the Lord first in my life blessed Metrohome, which grew rapidly.

We three from left to right: (me) Jack Welch, Jon Sopher, and Jon Knudson

When the Lord changed my heart, he used my business gifts effectively. Profits from Metrohome exceeded ten times what they were with CBS Homes.

The Honor and the Glory Go to the Lord, Not Me!

I was reminded of the Bible story about the rich man, Job, who lost everything but refused to deny the Lord! During his grief, his strong faith continued, and the Lord eventually blessed Job with ten times more than what he originally had.

I sold Metrohome to Scott Flatten and his wife Carolyn, who continued to operate under the Metrohome name as well as Award Homes by Metrohome in Rochester, Minnesota.

The business is described on the Metrohome website this way:

Over the past 25 years every home designed and built by Metrohome is an original, with its own elegance and character. We design and build each customer's home in the same uncompromising manner in which we would build our own. The commitment to quality is reflected, not just in the materials used in our homes, but also in the attitudes of those individuals that

make up our team of staff, subcontractors, and suppliers.

Because of Metrohome's commitment to the highest standards, our meticulous attention to detail and our determination to give each client the personal attention they deserve, Metrohome can achieve results that far exceed the ordinary and build a home of uncompromising quality.

The Lord provided the income for us to purchase a Skipperliner Houseboat in 2001. We shared the boat with our family and friends from 2001 until 2013, when we sold it. Wonderful memories were created on our boat. Its name, The New Life, was meant to start a conversation about faith.

Chapter 13

Medical Challenges

L ike so many people in our 70s and 80s, I've had my
share of medical problems, including "near misses"
that reminded me that our lives on this earth are very
fragile.

On February 15, 2006, I was shoveling snow in our
driveway, after a 12-inch snowstorm. It was the kind
of heavy, wet snow that is just right for causing a heart
attack, which it did.

I, of course, was determined to finish the job, something I never gave up on, no matter what the task was.
As I finished, I felt terrific chest pain. I struggled to get
the front door open and then collapsed on the floor in
a fetal position. Jann took one look at me, gave me two
aspirin and called 911. The wait seemed like an eternity
to Jann, who had grabbed her purse and coat and was
ready to go once the ambulance arrived.

The La Crescent Rescue Squad arrived first and quickly started CPR. The ambulance came soon after, putting me on a stretcher while Jann rode in front seat.

With that heavy snow, it took longer to get to the hospital. The attending heart surgeon operated as quickly as possible, but I did suffer some damage to my heart. Had I been able to reach the hospital 20 minutes earlier, he said he could have saved more of the muscle in my left ventricle.

Despite the seriousness of that heart attack, I was home within a week and recovered nicely.

The Lord saved me again!

My next medical misadventure came on the weekend of the summer of 2007 when our church celebrated its 75th anniversary. We had an open house on our houseboat for returning pastors and friends. Late Saturday afternoon I developed such intense pain in my abdomen that Jann rushed me to emergency room. Two doctors checked me over and sent me home. After being in severe pain all night, Jann brought me back to the emergency department early Sunday morning.

An x-ray showed I had a twisted bowel requiring emergency surgery as soon as possible. But it couldn't be done immediately because I took blood thinner since my heart surgery. They needed to thicken my blood so I wouldn't bleed to death on the operating table.

Once it was safe to operate, the surgeon removed three feet of colon and my gallbladder. Two nights later, I developed such severe pain at 2 a.m. that I called Jann and told her, "I'm dying! Come quickly! They are taking me back to surgery!"

My room was full of doctors and nurses all talking about what needed to be done. When my blood pressure dropped suddenly, they tipped my bed to get blood to flow to my brain. Jann arrived just as I left for surgery.

After the operation, I went to intensive care to be monitored closely. The doctor told me that my bowel had ruptured before surgery. This meant he had to perform an ileostomy and I had to wear a pouch on my right side to gather my stool.

When the surgeon said, "He was not sure I would make it through the night", Jann called friends and pastors to pray for me to live and be healed. Many came to pray with Jann for my recovery during the next few weeks. She stayed in the intensive care waiting room and would come in and see me at least twice per hour. Finally, I was able to move to a regular hospital room to continue my recovery.

It was not so easy, however. During my stay I developed a MRSA infection. MRSA stands for methicillin resistant staphylococcus aureus. It is a deadly staph infection that takes very strong antibiotics to fight it as it is resistant to many antibiotics.

During my hospital stay, staff inserted a drain below my ileostomy to remove the poison from my system. I was sent to a nursing home, where I stayed for nearly a year. Many weekends I was so weak they took me back to the hospital for IVs and feeding tubes.

My ileostomy had a high volume output so it was hard for me to keep weight on, let alone gain it. When I was finally able to get home, I was down to 120 pounds from my normal weight of 190 pounds on my once 6-foot-1-inch frame.

My clinic visits were often during my recovery. In the spring of 2009, my doctor suggested reconnecting my bowel back to normal. He asked me what doctor I wanted for the operation. When I suggested he be the surgeon, he told me he did not want to do the surgery himself because we had become good friends. "I don't want to lose you on the operating room table," he told me. In the end, he said he would operate under one condition: that he brings in another surgeon to assist him.

Jann, our friends and family continued praying for my surgery to be successful and without complications.

The Lord saved me again!

I think of Proverbs 3: 5-6:

"Trust in the Lord with all your heart, lean not onto your own understanding, but in all ways acknowledge him and he will straighten your path!"

I thank the Lord for the miracle he performed through the surgery. I was so elated by my recovery. No longer did I have to change the ileostomy bag hourly. We take for granted the functioning of the human body and God's creativity. What a marvelous creation we are.

The meaning of it all

During all of my illnesses I had no fear of surgery or dying; instead, I had great faith in God's outcome for me.

I recall my earlier days when my dad showed me the small lot in La Crescent where we would build our lumberyard. Despite my concerns, he said, "We are going to build it on faith."

And we did.

The small lot eventually **grew to 3-1/2 acres under roof or about 152,460 square feet.** Our business became the largest component home manufacturer in the Midwest.

Praise the Lord!

What is faith!!

"Faith is the substance of things hoped for and the evidence of things not seen." **Hebrews 11:1, New King James Version.**

As I look back on my life, certain things stand out in particular:

- I abused the inherent gifts the Lord gave me to satisfy my personal desires.
- Consolidated Builders Supply (our lumberyard) grew from nothing to Component Building Systems (CBS Homes). "
- As the business grew, **"I"** became most important, at least in my own life. **My wine, women and song** period was a bad time in my life. With my sin-sickened heart, I felt guilty, ashamed and had an emptiness. During this time, people looked up to me, not knowing who I really was inside.

It took my best friend **asking me to pray with him as he was dying from cancer to change** me. **Christ died on** the cross for my past, present and future sins. When I became a believer, my sins were forgiven and forgotten.

The following are some of the **Bible passages that have been most helpful**; AS I ROSE FROM THE ASHES:

- **"God shows his love for us in this: While we are still sinners, Christ died for us ... the free gift of God is eternal life in Christ Jesus Our Lord."** Romans 5:8 and 6:23.

- **"Christ Died for our sins ... he was buried ... he was raised on the third day."** I Corinthians 15: 3-4.

  God has provided the only way to forgiveness of sin and eternal life. We all have a choice to accept Jesus or reject Jesus in our life.

- **Jesus says, "I am the way, and the truth, and the life. No one comes to the Father except through me."** John 14:6

- The Bible says, **"Whoever believes in the Son has eternal life, but whoever rejects the Son will not see life, for God's wrath remains on them"** John 3:36

How do you find Jesus and become a beliver? I suggest you repeat this prayer:

Dear Jesus, thank you for making it possible for me to find peace with God! I believe that when you died, you were paying the penalty for my sins. I now receive you into my life as my Savior, so I can have forgiveness and never ending life from God! Thank you for the gift of eternal life! In Jesus name, Amen.

How do I know that I am saved and have eternal life!!: 1ˢᵗ John Chapter 5: Verse 13

<u>These things I have written unto you that believe on the name of the Son of God; that you may know that you have eternal life, and you may believe on the name of the Son of God.</u> (KJV)

As I grew in the Lord, my whole perspective in business changed as well. The **"I"** in my business became **"we."** The Lord was now the head and I was his servant. When I die, I now know I have eternal life with him. John 3:16.

I look back to the fire and discover the millions I lost are now a gain in finding Christ.

It is my hope that in reading my book, you will find blessings and peace!

The following pictures were taken at the Waterfront in La Crosse, Wisc. On Jack and Jann's

50ᵗʰ Anniversary June 21, 2008

Note

23 Terry Rindfleisch, "CBS Homes struggles for survival," *La Crosse Tribune*, January 1981

Back row, from left, are Jon and Bergen Sopher, Jacob, Brent and Ryan Welch. Middle row, from left, are Kendra and Kyleigh Sopher; and Jessica, Marianne, Kristin and James Welch. Front row from left, Andrew Sopher, Jack Welch, Natalie Sopher, and Nathaniel, Jann and Neona Welch. Family photo from 2008.

This 2008 photo shows our grandchildren and the grandchildren of my sister Cynthia Good. Back row, from left, are Kyleigh Sopher, Bergen, Jessica, Ryan and Jacob Welch; and Aleesha and Megan Good. Middle row, from left, are Andrew Sopher, Daniel Good, Natalie Sopher, and Neona Welch. Front row, from left are Sarah Good, Jack, Jann and Nathaniel Welch; and Hannah Good.

Activities and Awards

Community

- President, La Crescent Ski Club.
- Delegate to Minnesota State Republican Convention.
- American Legion Building Committee in 1969.
- Chairman of La Crosse Business and Professional Couples Club.
- Committee member for Building La Crescent High School and the La Crescent City Recreation Board of Directors.
- Donated CBS Homes' forklifts to use in building football field and bleachers for the high school.
- Chairman of La Crescent Swimming Pool Referendum, 1972 and 1973.
- Chairman of the Committee to Build Tennis Courts in La Crescent.
- Thirty-second Degree Shriner and Mason

- President and board member of La Crescent Chamber of Commerce
- President and board member of La Crescent Apple Festival

Bethany Church

- Co-chairman of Church Land Purchase Committee.
- Chair of Building Committee.
- Chair and Member of Board of Deacons.
- Adult Sunday teacher.
- Twenty-year member of Church Building Committee.
- Member of the Overseer Board.
- Past member of Board of Trustees.
- Project coordinator for church addition.

Professional

- Helped start La Crosse Area Home Builders with Harley Gibbons, charter member in 1967.
- Builder of the Year selected by the La Crosse Area Home Builders.
- People's Choice Award for a Parade Home.
- Board member of Houston County Home Builders Association.

- Elected to State of Minnesota Building Code Committee.
- Member of National Association of Home Builders.
- Member of National Component Home Manufacturing Association.
- CBS Homes was National Test Center for Bostitch Air Nailing and Stapling Equipment Tools.

Honors

- Listed in Who's Who in the Midwest.
- Listed in Notable Americans
- La Crescent Man of the Year.
- Awarded Life Membership in La Crosse Area Builders Association.
- 1976 Minnesota Chamber of Commerce Awarded CBS HOMES the second best business in the State of Minnesota (first place was Awarded to Rose Totina Pizza)

Acknowledgments

N o book is every written without the support and
assistance of many, including:

- My wife Jann, who stayed by my side when
  I was in my darkest time and for being so
  supportive throughout the years of our marriage. Her patient help was essential in creating this book.
- My children, their spouses, and my grandchildren who have heard many of these stories before and still appreciate them. I am
  grateful they have made Christ the center of
  their lives.
- Bethany Evangelical Free Church pastors
  and congregation members for their many
  prayers when I was ill spiritually and ill
  physically.
- Our many friends, who supported our family
  in good times and bad.

- Betty Kathan, the wife of my friend, Dick Kathan, who suggested *"UP FROM ASHES"* as the book title.
- La Crescent Historical society, for sharing historic photos.
- The *La Crosse Tribune,* which allowed me to use the front-page image from the devastating January 18, 1980, CBS Homes Fire. Ken Bernstein of River City Image Works added the color to the photo, which helps demonstrate the drama of that night.
- Susan T. Hessel and Gayda Hollnagel, who helped craft the book.
- Xulon Press for helping in publishing the book and spreading the word about a redeeming life.